KNIFE SKILLS

An Illustrated Kitchen Guide
to Using the Right Knife the Right Way

Bill Collins

D1468604

Storey Publishing

*The mission of Storey Publishing is to serve our customers by
publishing practical information that encourages
personal independence in harmony with the environment.*

Edited by Margaret Sutherland and Mollie Firestone
Series and cover design by Alethea Morrison
Art direction by Cynthia N. McFarland
Text production by Theresa Wiscovitch
Indexed by Christine R. Lindemer, Boston Road Communications

Cover illustration by © Lisel Ashlock
Interior illustrations by © Randy Glass Studio

Storey books are available for special premium and promotional uses and for
customized editions. For further information, please call 1-800-793-9396.

Storey Publishing
210 MASS MoCA Way
North Adams, MA 01247
www.storey.com

Printed in the United States by McNaughton & Gunn, Inc.
10 9 8 7 6 5 4 3 2 1

Library of Congress Cataloging-in-Publication Data

Collins, Bill, author, 1958– .
  Knife skills : a storey basics title / by Bill Collins.
     pages cm
  Includes index.
  ISBN 978-1-61212-379-0 (pbk. : alk. paper)
  ISBN 978-1-61212-380-6 (ebook) 1. Knives. 2. Cutlery. I. Title.
TX657.K54C65 2014
642'.7—dc23
                              2014015169

For my wife, Karen, who stayed with me even though the first things I ever cooked for her were kosher hot dogs

CONTENTS

When my grandmother was 83 years old, I was standing with her in her brother Joe's kitchen. I was a mere 22 years old and was trying to prepare dinner. Uncle Joe's knives were so dull that they would've had a tough time cutting through butter. I remembered that old saying, "The only thing more dangerous than a sharp knife is a dull knife." The implication is that you have to press harder with a dull knife, and that you'll probably slip and end up cutting yourself.

So I turned to my grandmother and was sure I could show off how smart I was. "Gramma," I said, "do you know what's more dangerous than a sharp knife?" She answered right back, "A woman's tongue." I said, "Umm, no, it's a dull knife," and I explained why. I was all set to claim victory when she looked at me and said, "That may be true, but there's nothing more dangerous than a woman's tongue."

The moral of the story? Never try to get cute with a short, sharp-tongued Cockney grandmother. It will always end badly.

INTRODUCTION

During the hundreds of classes and cooking demonstrations that I've taught over the years, the topic that I'm asked about more than any other is knives. People have questions about what types of knives to buy, how to use them, how to keep them sharp, and more. And I discovered something along the way: it's people's concerns and questions about their knife skills that prevent them from becoming more confident cooks. I've met many cooks who make terrific food but then tell me how stressed and nervous they are with their knives.

Well, help has arrived and you're reading it right now. This book will give you the confidence to choose and use the knives and other nonelectric sharp tools in your kitchen. It's also a reference book that you can use as you improve your skills and acquire the tools that will make you a better cook!

Most kitchens are filled with tools and gadgets that range from the most basic things that you need to cook to frivolous items that you never actually use. How do you decide which tools you need and want? How do you use them? And how do you take care of them so they'll last, in some cases, forever? This book will answer those questions so you won't end up with "it seemed like a good idea" things filling your kitchen drawers. Whether you're a new or experienced cook, I can guide you through the maze of knives and other sharp tools. I can help you become a better, more confident cook by choosing the tools that suit your needs and budget.

HOW TO CHOOSE AND USE YOUR KNIVES

Knives are the most important tools in your kitchen. Without them, all you can do is eat oatmeal, bananas, and take-out food. Choosing the right knives is crucial. What knives do you absolutely need? And what other knives do you want after you have the basics covered?

At the bare minimum, you need to have two knives: a chef's knife for cutting, chopping, and slicing, and a paring knife for the smaller tasks. The differences between these two knives are reflected in their size and the size of the food you're cutting. A chef's knife is so large that you wouldn't be able to get the fine movements needed to take the top off a strawberry without risking some damage to your fingers. And if you were to try to carve a turkey with a paring knife, you and your guests might have to wait a long time before dinner is served.

THE "FOUR AND A HALF" essential knives, (a) chef's knife, (b) offset handle serrated deli knife, (c) utility knife, (d) paring knife, and (e) bench scraper.

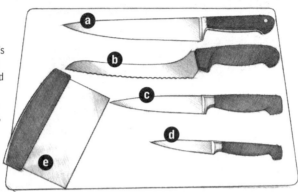

Together, these two knives meet the minimum requirements for you to be a confident cook.

But to help make cooking easier and more efficient, I think every cook needs "four and a half" knives. Along with the chef's knife and paring knife, these include a 6-inch utility knife, an offset handle serrated deli knife, and a bench scraper (which is what I refer to as half a knife). Any knives beyond these are task specific and will help you as your skills and collection of recipes grow.

But wait.

Some people would put one more knife into this must-have category: a Japanese Santoku knife. Many people use this knife instead of a chef's knife. Its shape and thin blade are ideal for slicing fruit and vegetables.

Japanese
Santoku knife

CHEF'S KNIFE

THE CHEF'S KNIFE WILL be your go-to knife for the vast majority of your cutting, chopping, slicing, and dicing. With it you can carve meat and poultry, chop onions, slice tomatoes, and mince cilantro and parsley. Plus a whole lot more.

Chef's knives generally come in three sizes: 8, 10, and 12 inches. The most popular size is the 8-inch knife. Many people feel a larger knife is too big, and that it will be less safe and effective to use. But if you hold your knife correctly and follow the chef's knife techniques, you'll find that a 10-inch chef's knife is more efficient, less tiring, and safer to use than an 8-inch one.

This might seem contradictory, as it seems like you will need more effort to control a longer knife. But, if you're slicing an onion, or almost any food, your arm and wrist will have to lift higher with a shorter blade. That's because chef's knives have an area that's used most effectively for slicing and chopping. It's like the "sweet spot" on a tennis racquet, golf club, or a baseball or cricket bat. On the chef's knife, this is toward the back half of the blade. This is where the weight of the knife,

THE PARTS OF A CHEF'S KNIFE

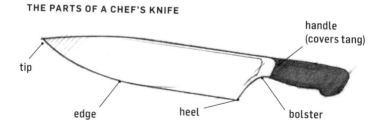

tip

handle
(covers tang)

edge

heel

bolster

combined with your effort, gives you the most effective cutting area. A shorter knife has a smaller sweet spot, and it must be lifted higher for that area to cut the food. As a result, the area that actually cuts the food is smaller. This puts more strain on your wrist, arm, and shoulder. For the same cutting results, with an 8-inch chef's knife, you have to work harder. And for a longer period of time too.

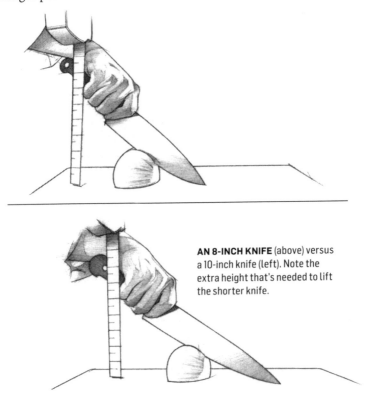

AN 8-INCH KNIFE (above) versus a 10-inch knife (left). Note the extra height that's needed to lift the shorter knife.

How to Hold a Chef's Knife

While it's important to be able to cut your food as you want, it's even more important to do it safely so you'll end up with as many fingers and thumbs as when you started the day. Remember, you want to cut your food, not your fingers.

Let's start with the knife hand. The first illustration on the next page shows the correct method; the next two illustrations show comfortable but unsafe ways to hold a knife.

The illustration showing knuckles under the handle highlights two problems. With the knife held this way, your knuckles will hit against the cutting board. This gets painful after a while. The second problem is that holding your knife like this means that you don't have full lateral control of your knife. This will cause your knife to wiggle from side to side. In the illustration with the index finger extended, you probably won't hit your knuckles on the board but you'll still have poor lateral control of the knife. If you are cutting something hard, like a carrot, the knife will probably slip a little. Or a lot.

The illustration with the thumb and forefinger held at the beginning of the blade, almost pinching it, shows how to have complete control of the knife, including lateral control. Not only will this reduce your chances of cutting yourself, but it will also actually require less effort for you to cut the food. That's because the knife is going exactly where you want it to go while being held firmly, without slipping, in your hand.

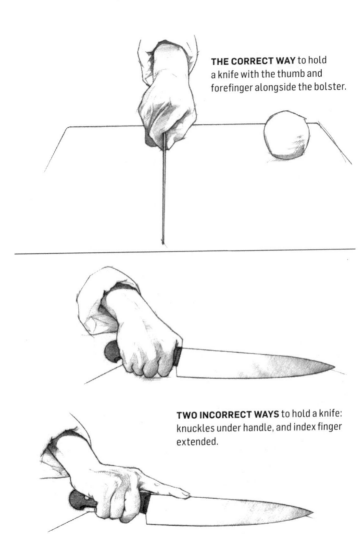

THE CORRECT WAY to hold a knife with the thumb and forefinger alongside the bolster.

TWO INCORRECT WAYS to hold a knife: knuckles under handle, and index finger extended.

On the Other Hand

Both hands play a role in how to use a chef's knife, as well as all other knives. The hand not holding the knife, called the guide hand, is very important because it's holding and guiding the food being cut.

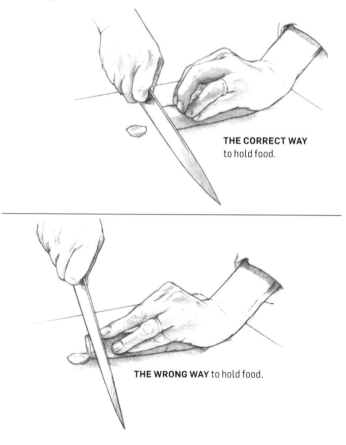

THE CORRECT WAY to hold food.

THE WRONG WAY to hold food.

The first illustration on page 9 shows the correct and safe way to hold the food, with your fingers almost standing up. This forms a shield, or barrier, when you're cutting the food. Plus, it removes your fingertips from being anywhere near the knife's blade. Since there's rarely a time when you need to pick your knife tip up from the cutting board, your knife will not be rising above your bent fingers. Which means you won't cut them. The one problem with doing it this way is that it feels awkward and unnatural until you've practiced it for a while.

The second illustration shows the wrong way to hold the food being cut, with the hand resting in a natural position. Most people hold their food like this for two reasons: it's more comfortable, and they've been doing it this way forever. The problem with this technique is that it exposes all of your fingers to being cut when the knife slips. Not *if* the knife slips. *When* the knife slips.

Basic Chef's Knife Techniques

Sliding and chopping are the two basic chef's knife techniques. The sliding technique is used to cut and slice food such as onions, scallions, and carrots. The knife slides forward while cutting, and is pulled back, above or away from the food, to slice again. Note how the tip of the knife stays on the cutting board.

The second technique is used to chop herbs or mince food that's already been cut, such as onions or garlic. One hand holds the knife as the other hand rests on top of the knife near the end of the blade. Picture the face of a clock. The knife then pivots while chopping, going from approximately 4:00 to 5:00

(maybe 3:30 to 5:30), and back again, to continuously chop the food smaller and smaller. A large mound of parsley sprigs will be reduced to small bits of minced parsley in less than a minute by using this technique.

Both techniques have one thing in common: the tip of the chef's knife does not leave the cutting board while you're cutting, slicing, or chopping. This is important because many people are under the impression that lifting the knife in the air while cutting and chopping is faster, more efficient, and cool looking. It's none of these. Every time you lift your knife off the board, you are losing some control over it. Keeping the tip on the board allows you to begin your motion where you want it to be. If you start, or continue, to have the knife in the air before cutting into the food, then the knife won't go exactly where you want it to go. It might go there. But not every time. And not safely.

MINCING CILANTRO using the chopping technique.

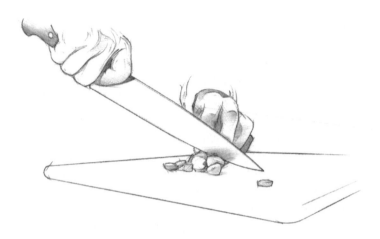

SLICING CARROTS using the sliding knife technique.

Santoku Knives . . . the Other Chef's Knife?

The Santoku knife (page 4) has gained popularity in recent years and many home cooks use it, rather than a chef's knife, for most of their everyday tasks. But while a Santoku knife has many great attributes, especially as a slicer, it lacks the versatility of a chef's knife. When you safely use a chef's knife, you rarely have to lift it from the cutting board. It's easier on the arm and shoulder, with the board taking much of the impact and weight of the work. Because the Santoku is much shorter than a chef's knife, it cannot be used with the same comfort and efficiency. You'd have to constantly lift the knife off the cutting board because it is too short to slide back and forth like a chef's knife. The difference in length also means that you cannot slice and chop in the same volume as a chef's knife without increased fatigue and a decrease in accuracy. Plus, more of the effort of your work will go from the knife to your arm and shoulder.

I do like the Santoku knife. But I think of it as a hybrid between the 6-inch utility knife and a chef's knife rather than a replacement. There are enough differences and similarities between chef's knives and Santoku knives to make the Santoku a valuable addition to your collection of regularly used cutlery. The biggest difference, which makes the Santoku so valuable, is its stability and effectiveness as a slicer for so many foods including carrots, onions, tomatoes, and raw chicken breast.

PARING KNIFE

THE PARING KNIFE (page 4) is the second most important knife to have, if for no other reason than it can do the small tasks for which the chef's knife is too big. Why would a chef's knife be too big for a job? Take an onion, for example. While a chef's knife is pointy and sharp enough to take the root end out of an onion, your hand will be so far away that you really won't have the control to make the small, fine cuts as you would with the paring knife. You'd be more likely to cut your hand than the onion.

What tasks does the paring knife do best? Paring is defined as the act of cutting away an edge or a surface. While this would imply a vegetable peeler, it's more than that. With a sharp paring knife you can easily peel an apple, tomato, or orange. You can use it to hull strawberries, remove the core from tomatoes and onions, and slice the segments out of a piece of citrus with a supreme cut (see Preparing Fruit, page 97). It's also a perfect knife for slicing salamis and many cheeses. You can even peel a grape with a paring knife.

Not all paring knives look the same. Their blades can be between 2 and 4 inches long, and some blades are curvier than others. And unlike other types of knives, you don't always have to use a cutting board when using a paring knife. The tasks are often too small, and too close, to be accurate and efficient on a cutting board. As long as you take your time and don't direct the knife toward you, you can safely and comfortably hold and turn the food in your guide hand. Depending on the task, you may hold the paring knife in one hand while keeping the thumb of your knife hand on the food. It's more about the comfort level with the task, which you do slowly, rather than the method used, as with the chef's knife.

THREE DIFFERENT WAYS TO HOLD A PARING KNIFE

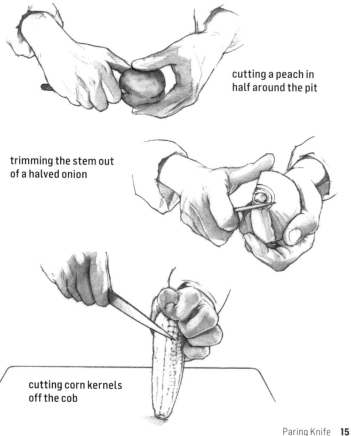

cutting a peach in half around the pit

trimming the stem out of a halved onion

cutting corn kernels off the cob

UTILITY KNIFE

THE UTILITY KNIFE (page 4) is used less often than the paring knife, but it plays the role of the in-between knife. It does those odd tasks that are too small for the chef's knife and too big for the paring knife, like taking the core out of a cabbage (or a cauliflower). To do so, pierce the cabbage and carefully move the knife slowly alongside the core. After each downward slice — with your guide hand on the cabbage above the knife, out of the path of the blade — stop, rotate the cabbage a quarter turn, and slice again. Repeat. This is a slow process, as the core can be quite dense. If you try to do this quickly, then your knife will probably slip and the tip can break off.

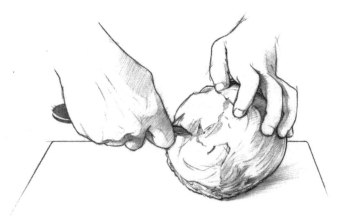

CORING A CABBAGE with a utility knife.

Other uses for a utility knife include carving roasted poultry or cutting the ends off onions, then peeling them. Or, it might be the knife closest at hand, and you want to slice a tomato or cut the peel and pith (the white inner layer) off an orange. It's also very good for slicing small blocks of cheese.

OFFSET HANDLE SERRATED DELI KNIFE

THE OFFSET HANDLE SERRATED DELI KNIFE (page 4) is the least known of all these knives. It's also the most versatile. The benefits of this knife come from both the blade and the handle. Serrated knives have more pronounced teeth on their blades than most other knives. The large teeth allow the knife to literally get a grip on the food before cutting it while other knives start sliding immediately. This allows you to cut foods with odd-textured crusts and skins that often seem to fight back with regular knives. Ideal tasks include slicing crusty breads, cutting the outer skin off melons and other large fruit, slicing tomatoes, and cutting sandwiches and bagels.

As the blade cuts right through these irregular surfaces, the offset handle allows your knuckles to avoid hitting either the cutting board or the counter. I never used an offset handle serrated knife until after I graduated from cooking school. I'm not sure I'd even seen one. I had used regular handle serrated knives before on bread and tomatoes. I still have two or three of them stashed away in a cabinet. As I mentioned earlier, if you're not comfortable with a knife, then you won't use it.

That idea hadn't dawned on me until I realized that I wasn't using my serrated knives at all.

So how can an oddly shaped handle change a knife from being discarded to being so valuable? It's my knuckles. And your knuckles too. As with a badly held chef's knife, the regular handle serrated knife, with its narrow handle and blade, doesn't allow room for your knuckles to clear the cutting board while slicing tomatoes and bread.

The offset handle serrated deli knife isn't perfect. Because its teeth are so large, it's very difficult to sharpen this knife. Most home sharpening tools cannot sharpen a serrated blade, and many sharpening professionals can't do it either. Although it doesn't need to be sharpened as often as other knives, you shouldn't overspend when buying this knife. When it gets too dull after a few years, or more, of use, then buy a new one. It's a small price to pay for such a versatile knife.

SLICING A TOMATO with a deli knife.

BENCH SCRAPER

WHEN I SUGGESTED THAT YOU needed four and a half knives, it's the bench scraper that I consider to be the equivalent of half a knife. Although the bench scraper is technically not a knife, it's too important to be excluded. Its original function was for pastry chefs to cut and divide dough, and to scrape the sticky remains of dough off the work surface. But its everyday use has much more value than just baking. Its best use is to transfer the food you've just cut from your cutting board to a bowl or directly into the pan.

If it's not your habit to use a bench scraper, then you're probably using the side of your knife's blade to scoop up the food off your cutting board. Or even using your hands cupped together. These methods can often lead to multiple tries to get

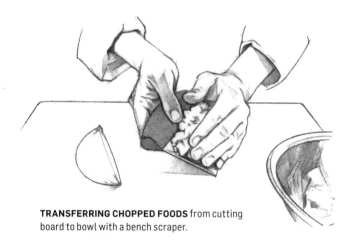

TRANSFERRING CHOPPED FOODS from cutting board to bowl with a bench scraper.

all of the chopped food to its destination. With the flat, wide bench scraper, it's rare that even the largest mound of chopped food needs more than two or three tries to clear the board. It turns a task that often spills food on the counter and floor into a quick and easy step. I always keep a bench scraper by the side of my cutting board whenever I'm cooking. It's like an extension of my hand. And it almost always costs less than $10.

OPTIONAL KNIVES

THE OPTIONAL KNIVES ARE the ones you'll use for nondaily tasks.

Boning Knife

A boning knife is almost misnamed. Its name implies that it cuts through bones. Actually, it has two main functions, and I've added a third. But none of these functions include cutting through bones.

Its main functions are to cut around bones and to get in between joints to separate them. For instance, if you want to separate a chicken into individual pieces (such as leg, thigh, and breast), a boning knife will help you move around the bones more finely and easily. A boning knife is much narrower than a chef's or utility knife, which means you can maneuver around the meat and bones with more precision and cut exactly where you want to cut. The larger knives are too wide to give you that flexibility. The same is true with beef or other meats, if you need to trim them or separate them into their individual ribs.

Boning knives come in two types: a flexible and nonflexible blade. If you're going to buy just one boning knife, get the one that's flexible. This will allow the blade to more easily adjust to the contours of the meat. Which brings up the third, lesser-known function of a boning knife: to remove things like fat, gristle, and silver skin from meat. The narrowness of the blade allows you to make small cuts and slices to remove even the smallest imperfections from the meat.

How important is it to have a boning knife? Well, here's why this is one of the optional knives: it's time to buy one if you are doing increasingly more boning of meats, poultry, and fish, and you're not getting the precision and speed that you'd like with a different knife. Yes, you can get the same accuracy with another knife. But it will take you much longer to do it. The knife will pay for itself if you decide to buy whole chickens, rather than the more expensive individual parts. With just a bit of practice, you can cut up the chicken quickly and easily, and save money at the same time.

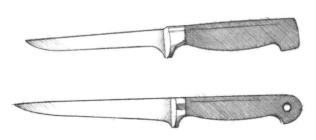

BONING KNIVES with nonflexible (top) and flexible (bottom) blades.

A boning knife is used for raw meat. If you use it for slicing cooked meat, you'll find that it's too short, narrow, and curved to function effectively.

Fillet Knife

A fillet knife is similar to a boning knife, but it has a longer and slightly narrower blade, and is used almost exclusively on fish. When the word *fillet* is used with meat, it's used as a noun. But when it's used with fish, it's both a noun ("fillet of fish") and a verb ("fillet that fish"). No one ever says, "fillet that cow."

....

How Do You Get to Carnegie Hall? Practice!

There is a big challenge in teaching new knife techniques to experienced cooks. From my classes where experienced cooks have told me that they're uncomfortable with their knife skills, the dilemma comes with learning these new techniques. In some cases, people have been uncomfortable with their own knife skills for decades. To them, I have one word of advice: practice! The difficulty is not with their knife hand. That technique is easier to remember and use. The difficulty is with the guide hand. It's unnatural to stand your fingers up on the food. This takes practice. When I was in cooking school, it took me three months before I started to place my fingers safely in that position without having to remind myself. So, give yourself some time to get used to it until one day, you realize that you did this out of habit, and not because you needed a reminder. Your fingers will thank you.

....

Steak Knives

Many years ago, it wasn't unusual for people to get their steak knives from either gas stations or S&H Green Stamps. Gas stations were a popular place to receive the knives as a reward for buying your gas for 25 cents per gallon. For many decades, S&H Green Stamps were the equivalent of credit card rewards points. Both of these knife sources highlight how unimportant steak knives were for many years. They were an afterthought in most homes.

However, steak knives have long been available everywhere knives are sold. From big-box stores to specialty shops, you can spend between $15 and $250 for four knives. If a lower-cost sharp steak knife can't easily cut your steak, you have two choices: more-expensive knives, or better-quality steak. My recommendation would be to upgrade your steak selection.

Slicer

The slicer has one function: to slice the meat or fish in one slicing motion. There is no back-and-forth motion needed for a slicer. The knife is very long, usually 12 inches, although shorter ones are available. It's most often seen in slicing the white (breast) meat off turkey, or carving thin slices off large cuts of beef. (See page 64 on how to carve and slice a turkey without using a slicer.)

Most slicers are used by food service professionals, as most people rarely have the volume of food that would necessitate a slicer. The slicing knife's blade is very thin and flexible, which allows for very thin slices. This is most visible in New York delicatessens serving beef brisket or corned beef, or sliced-to-order smoked salmon. It's been said that some longtime workers in New York delis can slice smoked salmon so thin that you could read a newspaper through it. That comes from years of practice, and a very sharp slicer.

Some slicing knives have rounded tips. These are seen mostly in restaurants that have carving stations. The rounded tip is a safety measure, to prevent customers from being jabbed when they, or the chef, lean too far forward to place the food on the plate with the knife under the food.

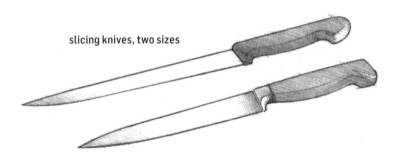

slicing knives, two sizes

Meat Cleaver

The function of the meat cleaver is to cut through bones, tendons, and very thick meat. It has a wide, thick, rectangular blade. And it's heavy. It can weigh more than a pound. Given its weight, size, and thickness, the meat cleaver's job is not fine slicing. Its job is to cut large pieces of meat and bones into smaller ones.

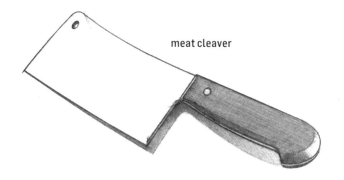
meat cleaver

Why not just use your chef's knife to cut through bones? Yes, a chef's knife can easily go through some bones, as with chicken or most fish. But beef bones in particular are very dense. You'd need very strong arms to cut through a beef bone with a chef's knife. The cleaver has the advantage of both its weight and momentum, because you swing it down from at least 12 to 18 inches above the cutting board to gain more heft in the cut.

Mezzaluna

A mezzaluna is a mostly single-purpose tool. Its use is for chopping herbs. With its rounded blade, it just needs a rocking motion, back and forth, to chop the herbs as finely as you'd like. Mezzalunas are available with either one or two blades. As a professional chef, I've never felt the need to use one. Herbs chop quite easily with a chef's knife. The main reason to buy a mezzaluna is if you're chopping a mountain of herbs every day. It will make your task easier and faster.

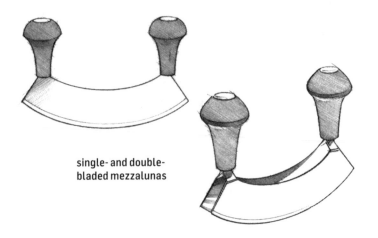

single- and double-
bladed mezzalunas

Oyster, Clam, and Scallop Knives

These knives are called shuckers, as are the people who use them. They're generally not very sharp (the knives, not the people). To use them, their dulled tips are wedged between the two halves of the shell to pry it open. The knives for shucking oysters, clams, and scallops are slightly different from each other. This is due to their respective shells being slightly different as well.

Don't be fooled into believing that injuring yourself on the dull edges of these knives isn't likely. Quite the opposite. It's extremely easy to stab your hand with a shucker. The most common way is when the knife slips as it's prying open a shell. Very often, it slips against the shell's irregular, wet surface. This is easy to do, especially if the shell isn't opening, or you don't easily find the little nook to use to leverage your shucker into opening the shell. It's a common sight to see someone quickly shucking oysters or clams at a raw bar. It's important to remember that the person doing the shucking has had lots of practice, and probably has many scars to show for it.

If you are going to shuck oysters, clams, or scallops, make sure you take your time. Don't try to do this if you're in a hurry. Be very patient. Also, hold the shell either with a towel, or even better, a Kevlar (or other cut-resistant) kitchen glove. You can still easily injure yourself, but the glove can help protect you against most of the slipping.

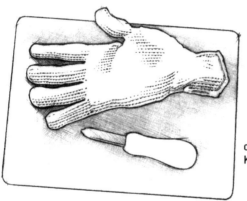

oyster knife and Kevlar glove

A Spoon

Yes, a spoon isn't sharp. And you can't cut yourself with one. But a spoon can peel two foods better than a knife: fresh ginger and kiwifruit.

To peel ginger, simply scrape its skin with the side of a teaspoon. Removing the skin with a spoon is faster, easier, and results in a higher yield than when using a knife. This is because ginger always has an irregular shape. If you do use a knife, then by the time you've trimmed it and cut off the peel, you've lost quite a bit of the ginger. And in the same amount of time, you'd have finished the task with a spoon.

Kiwifruit uses a different technique and spoon. Cut off the ends of the kiwifruit. Then, slip a tablespoon between the kiwifruit's flesh and skin. Gently rotate the spoon around the outside of the fruit. The skin will pop off, and you'll have a round, peeled kiwifruit. If you peel a kiwifruit with a knife, you probably won't end up with a smooth, round, peeled fruit. It'll have straight sides where you trimmed off the skin with your knife.

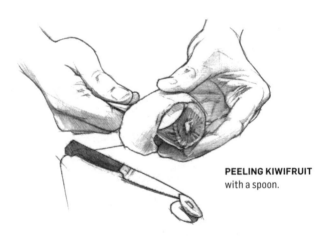

PEELING KIWIFRUIT
with a spoon.

CHAPTER TWO

HOW TO BUY A KNIFE

Now that you know how to hold and use a knife, how do you buy one? Other than handing over money, of course. Well, you have many options. Many people have rightly said that you should buy a knife that's comfortable in your hand. But what does that mean, and how do you find out if the knife is comfortable?

You can buy knives anywhere, including cutlery stores that specialize in selling knives, surplus/salvage stores, big-box stores, and online merchants. You can spend anywhere from $10 to over $200 for one knife. Or more. With such a range in shopping and prices, what are the deciding factors in buying a knife? Here are a few things to guide you. The knife should be:

1. Comfortable in your hand
2. A quality item
3. A fair price that fits your budget
4. Easily sharpened

COMFORT AND BALANCE

WHEN YOU BUY YOUR KNIVES, especially your chef's knife, it's crucial that your knife be comfortable for you. If it's not comfortable, you won't use it. It's that simple.

This is completely subjective and may be hardest to decide. What's comfortable for me might not be comfortable for you. My preference is a 10-inch chef's knife with a thin blade and no bolster. Why? Because it feels comfortable in my hand. When I hold the knife, the feel of the thinner blade between my thumb and forefinger is more comfortable than a wider blade with a bolster. While I do sometimes use knives with thicker blades, I'm more comfortable with a thinner one. There's no technical reason. The presence of a bolster means the blade will be thicker. Also, the length of the knife has no bearing on whether or not there's a bolster. That's a design choice of the manufacturer. This is why it's so important to hold a chef's knife before you buy it. You might like a bolster. You might not care. But it would be disappointing to bring home a knife only to find that you don't like using it.

Comfortable also means how the handle feels in your hand. You have at least four choices: a traditional wooden or wood composite handle found on European knives, a D-shaped handle, a molded plastic handle, or a handle that's sculpted from the same piece of metal that forms the blade. My preference is the traditional wood and wood composite handle. It feels more comfortable to me. But you might feel otherwise. This is where the place you buy your knife becomes important.

The knife also has to feel balanced. This too is completely personal and up to you. What does balanced mean? After determining that the handle is comfortable, this leaves the weight and tipping of the knife to be determined. When you hold it in the air, does it tip forward like it has too much weight in the blade? Does it tip backward, or lift up, because the handle feels too heavy and the blade feels too light?

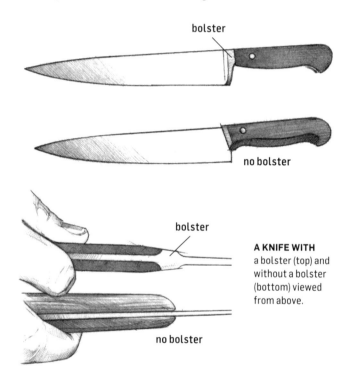

bolster

no bolster

bolster

no bolster

A KNIFE WITH a bolster (top) and without a bolster (bottom) viewed from above.

There's no formula or chart to match the handle and balance. It's solely a matter of what you like and feel. A knife might feel perfect to me, but not to you. So when you're knife shopping, hold as many knives as you possibly can (but not at once!), for two reasons: You'll have this knife forever. And you'll never use a knife that you don't like.

THE FOUR MAIN TYPES OF HANDLES

wood (or wood composite)

plastic

D-shaped

Japanese metal

WHERE TO BUY

STORES THAT SPECIALIZE IN KITCHEN KNIVES will offer many more knives, and more varieties of them. They offer expertise, service, information, and a chance for you to hold the knives in order to determine if they're comfortable. These stores include Williams-Sonoma, which has locations across the United States, and many other locally owned and nearby kitchenware stores across the country. At a specialty store, you'll have the opportunity to try the knives out on a countertop cutting surface. You can practice the cutting, slicing, and chopping techniques that you use in your kitchen. You'll be able to feel the different handle types and decide what feels comfortable. And the selection of knives will be much greater than anywhere else. Plus, you'll find that there's someone at the store who can spend the time to help you find the knife that's right for you. An added bonus is that most specialty knife stores offer sharpening services. If you choose not to sharpen your knives yourself, then this is a great, reliable service to have. The downside of a specialty knife store is the perception of higher prices.

At the other end of the buying experience are surplus or salvage stores. You'll usually find a limited selection of very inexpensive knives. Occasionally, you'll find a terrific knife that's vastly underpriced. But these deals are very rare. Surplus and salvage stores often have mystery knives. You don't always know the brand or the quality of the knife. It's likely that the knives you'll find are of a lesser quality than what you'd find in a knife specialty store or a big-box store.

You can also buy knives at big-box stores, which sell a limited selection of knives, often in sets that include basic knives, steak knives, scissors, and a knife storage block. The benefit of big-box stores is often in pricing. Boxed sets of multiple knives are usually featured. From reputable manufacturers, these can be a very good value. But since the knives are packaged to prevent mishaps, you can't hold the knives in your hand, try them for comfort, or see how they feel on a cutting board. This is one of the reasons they offer competitive pricing on their knives. Also, you may have to purchase multiple knives in a set to get the one or two that you really want.

Many of the knives at big-box stores are from reputable manufacturers, including Lamson, J. A. Henckels, Wüsthof, Messermeister, KitchenAid, Dexter-Russell, Victorinox, Forschner, Sabatier, and others. These are not cheap, poorly made knives. Many are very good and will last a long time. But sometimes a quality difference does exist between knives from a box store and those from a specialty store, even when they're from the same manufacturer. Does this mean that a Wüsthof knife from Target is inferior to the one from a local cutlery store? Not necessarily. It may be the same knife, or it may be different. This means that you have to ask about them at both stores. And if the knives are different, will this matter to you? This is something that only you can determine, on a knife-by-knife basis.

And finally, there's shopping online. Buying your knives online allows you to compare pricing and delivery times without having to leave your home or pajamas. For many people this is a huge benefit. But while online shopping may offer very competitive prices, it also takes away the option of holding the knife to see if it's comfortable. Or to even see, beyond its online picture, what it looks like.

Price

How much should you spend on your knife? After reviewing your needs, and then shopping around and trying to compare the various knives, you'll then find a whole range of prices. When you compare prices it'll seem as though you're comparing apples and chickens. You'll see different and similar metals, styles, and prices. And the level of service and help from the store, if you want it. How do you then make the most informed choice?

This is easy. Don't overthink it. You're buying something that will last you for many years. If you're uncomfortable with the price, then buy a less expensive one. But remember that a difference of $10, $20, or $50, over the life of the knife, is not a lot of money. If it's in your budget, then buy the knife that best suits your needs.

KNIFE QUALITY

BUT WHAT ABOUT QUALITY? How is quality defined in a knife? Years ago, all you needed to know about a knife was that it was German. This assured you that it was a quality knife that would stay sharp and last for years. But the rules have changed. Today, German knives and other European knives, as well as American knives, have good, as well as less-than-good, products. And Japanese knives are as good as everyone else's. Reputable Japanese knife manufacturers include Global, Shun, and Kyocera. The biggest difference is that traditional Western-style knives have thicker blades than the Japanese ones. This is most noticeable when you're slicing, whether it's an onion, carrot, or chicken breast. With a thicker blade, you can get a thin slice. But with the thinner blade, you can get a much thinner slice.

Another old rule was that a forged knife was much better than a stamped one. A forged knife is made from a single piece of metal and is created, with great care, one at a time. A stamped knife is mechanically cut from a large piece of metal. Actually, many are cut and shaped at once, and then sharpened, polished, and their handles attached. The old rule was firm: a forged knife was much better than a stamped one. It would hold its edge longer, and last longer. One advantage of holding an edge longer is that the knife will need less sharpening, and will not be ground down, literally, with years of consistent sharpening. But the quality of stamped knives has vastly improved. There is no reason that a stamped knife won't also give you many years of solid and comfortable use. Which means that if a knife feels comfortable and balanced in your hand, then you should buy it.

The vast majority of today's kitchen knives are made out of high carbon stainless steel. The advantage of these knives, since they became the standard material for knives approximately 40 years ago, is that they won't rust. This was a problem with previous knives. Currently, though, high carbon stainless steel is a bit softer than the old steel, which means these knives need to be sharpened more often. They still hold their edges well. Just not as long.

A never-ending debate topic is the differences in quality between Japanese and German steel. The quality of both is terrific. The German steel is well suited to their wider style of blades. And the Japanese steel is well suited to their thinner, shorter style of blades. The decision comes down to what style of knife you want and need. The quality of the steel is no longer an issue at all. The only issue, once you decide on the type of knife you need, is its comfort in your hand.

Ceramic Knives

Ceramic knives are a recent addition to the knife world. Instead of steel, they are made out of a manufactured material that looks like, but isn't, plastic. Here's a comparison: a Japanese knife is light, while a ceramic knife is ultralight. The first time you use one, it'll feel like a toy. An extremely sharp toy. They come in many styles: paring, utility, Santoku, chef's, and more. And they're made all over the world, even though they have a Japanese look and feel to them.

Ceramic knives are useful for many tasks, such as cutting vegetables, fruit, and meat with no bones. They cut with more precision than the traditional Japanese knives. But they are also very flawed.

Ceramic knives tend to be brittle. They cannot take the heavy use of chopping and striking into the cutting board. It's not that they lose their sharpness this way. It's that their blades tend to break under what would be normal use with a nonceramic knife. Common tasks such as mashing garlic with the side of the blade, chopping at a slightly wrong angle, or even accidentally dropping the knife onto the floor can easily lead to breaking ceramic blades. You also don't want to cut into anything that might twist and then break the blade. Removing the core from a cabbage or trying to cut frozen, or semifrozen foods, can easily snap a ceramic blade. Even cutting a dense cheese can break a ceramic knife. I found this out the hard way, while cutting through a small wedge of Parmesan cheese.

You won't find any ceramic knives that have a warranty against breaking. But there are two things to look for if you do buy one. The first is that it comes with a sleeve to use when storing the knife. This will protect the blade from becoming damaged while being stored in a drawer. In rare instances, you can accidentally twist and break the blade when putting it into a knife block.

The other thing is to make sure you're allowed to return it to the manufacturer to be sharpened. They usually charge only for shipping and handling. But not every manufacturer offers this, so make sure it's stated on the package, or from the store where you're buying it. Very few retailers and businesses that do sharpening offer ceramic knife sharpening. While the blade will stay sharp for a very long time, when it does need sharpening, you definitely cannot do it yourself. Even better, some manufacturers will replace your knife, free of charge, if it's too dull or pitted to sharpen.

CHAPTER THREE

CARING FOR YOUR KNIVES

I have one simple rule for caring for knives: if you treat them well, they'll treat you well. And by treating you well, that means that they'll last for many years. My primary knives are over 20 years old, and should be going strong for many more years. You can get the same mileage out of yours by paying attention to how you wash, store, and use your knives.

WASHING AND STORING

ALWAYS WASH YOUR KNIVES BY HAND. Do not give in to the temptation of expediency by putting your knives in the dishwasher. Two bad things will happen. Not *might* happen. Will happen. The first is that over time, by soaking and steaming your knives in the long dishwasher cycle, water will get between the handle and the tang. This will eventually degrade the wood (or whatever material your knife handle is made from) and slowly separate it from the tang. Another problem with the dishwasher is that other dishes or glassware may also clank and bump against the knife blade. This can dull and damage your blade.

It's important to never put your knife in the sink unless you are going to wash it immediately. It's easy to forget that a sharp knife might be lurking among the dishes, or worse, submerged and soaking in soapy water. This is particularly problematic if someone else is washing the dishes and knives. It would be a very unpleasant surprise to reach into the sink and unknowingly grab the unfriendly end of the knife.

Storage Options

First and foremost, you want to store your knives safely so children cannot reach them. Once you've located a safe place to store your knives, you have three storage choices. The first is a knife block. This usually stays on the kitchen counter, as it puts the knives easily within reach when you're cooking. Many versions of knife blocks are available. Make sure your block has enough slots for all of your knives. Some blocks conveniently have slots at the bottom for steak knives. One helpful hint: If your knife block has vertical slots, you can place your knives in these slots with the sharp side up. This minor step may help keep your knives sharper for a longer period of time.

The second storage choice is in a drawer. Some knife blocks are designed to go into drawers instead of sitting on your countertop. This is especially helpful if your countertop space is

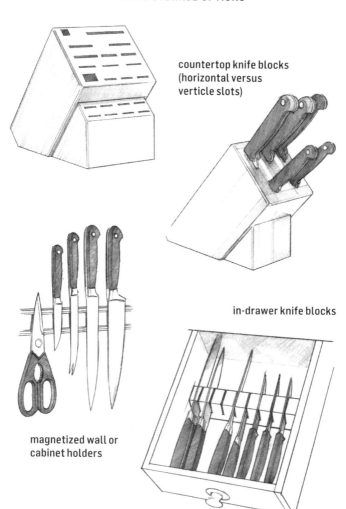

countertop knife blocks
(horizontal versus
verticle slots)

in-drawer knife blocks

magnetized wall or
cabinet holders

limited, or if you have plenty of drawer space. Another drawer storage option is to place plastic sleeves onto the knife blades to protect your knives and you. This is a good idea if you have just a few knives and very limited storage space. Do not place your knives in a drawer without protective sleeves or a knife block. This will certainly dull your knives quickly, and it will increase your chances of cutting your fingers when you reach into the drawer.

The third choice is magnetic strip holders. These mount on your wall or cabinet. A very strong magnet holds the blade in place, with the handle at the bottom, and the tip facing up. While these are very popular in commercial kitchens, magnetic holders are my least favorite way to store knives at home. A momentary slip can cause a knife to fall. Plus, some magnets require a bit of extra effort to remove a knife. Forcefully moving a knife can easily lead to an accident.

SHARPENING

THERE ARE USUALLY TWO QUESTIONS about knife sharpening: How often should it be done? What's the best way to do it?

Predicting the frequency of knife sharpening is like trying to figure out how far a car will go on a gallon of gas: your mileage may vary. That is, some people use their knives more often than others, or use cutting surfaces that might dull their blades. So, the simple answer is to sharpen your knives when they get dull.

As for the sharpening methods, if you ask five people their opinions on how to sharpen knives, you might get six answers. The options range from having a professional sharpen your knives to doing it yourself with a sharpening device or a whetstone.

Having your knives sharpened by someone who's a professional is almost always a good idea. This takes the worry and anxiety out of what can be a mysterious process. The only downside is going without your knives for anywhere from a day to a week, depending on who is doing the sharpening.

A variety of do-it-yourself sharpening devices are available. These are often called pull-through sharpeners, and come in electric and nonelectric styles. The decision of which one to buy rests on ease of use, your budget, and the recommendation of the person at the knife store. The benefit of these devices is clear: you get to sharpen your knives whenever it's needed. The disadvantage is that not all sharpening devices work easily and well. If you're not careful, you can damage your knives.

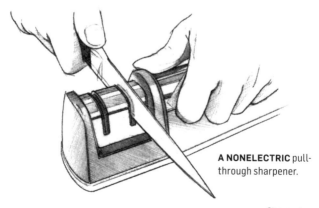

A NONELECTRIC pull-through sharpener.

What most of these devices have in common is that you slide your knife's blade through two V-shaped slots. One slot has a stone or two on a roller that sharpens the blade. The second slot hones, or fine-tunes, the blade.

Using a whetstone is the least expensive, and most daunting, of all home-sharpening devices. While some sharpening stones are wet from using oil on them, the word "whet" actually means "to sharpen." Since the time when we were living in caves, we have been sharpening all kinds of things on stones. Their abrasive surfaces have always been perfect to grind off just enough metal to give a very sharp edge. So what could possibly go wrong with this cost-effective method? While it's easy to sharpen a knife on a whetstone, it takes a bit of practice to get it right. You can end up with a knife that's duller than when you started. So what's the secret to using a whetstone? It's all in the angle of the knife on the stone. And practice.

How to Use a Whetstone

To sharpen your knife, you must slide the blade on the whetstone at a 22½-degree angle. There's a trick to figuring out this 22½-degree angle. First, hold your knife straight up with the sharp edge of the blade resting on the stone. This is a 90-degree angle. Tip the knife over onto one side, cutting the 90-degree angle in half. This is now 45 degrees. Then tip the knife again, cutting the 45-degree angle in half, and you're now at 22½ degrees. You're ready to start sharpening your knife.

Next is the motion for the sharpening technique. Hold your knife handle in one hand, with your other hand resting on the side of the blade. Slide the knife, from the handle end of the blade to the tip, along the whetstone. Repeat this on both sides until your knife is sharpened. Again, learning the correct motion will take some practice.

While you can get a very sharp edge on your blade, it will never be as sharp as it was on the day it left the factory. You can come close to this edge. But the manufacturing process is too precise to be duplicated.

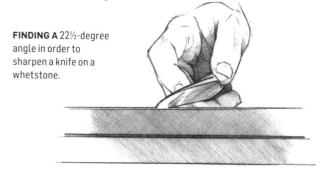

FINDING A 22½-degree angle in order to sharpen a knife on a whetstone.

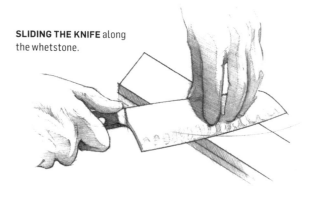

SLIDING THE KNIFE along the whetstone.

Sharpening Steel and Sharpening Diamond Steel

These two tools are very similar looking, but play different roles. The sharpening steel is smoother to the touch and is used primarily to make a sharp knife even sharper. It's advisable to use the steel often, perhaps even every time you use your knives, to help keep your knives sharp. Using a steel is unlike the steps of sharpening your knives, which removes bits of steel to bring back its edge. The sharpening steel actually rearranges and realigns the edge of the blade to keep it sharp. One thing it won't do is actually sharpen a dull blade. Its function is to make a sharp blade sharper. This process is also called "honing," and the tool is often called a honing steel.

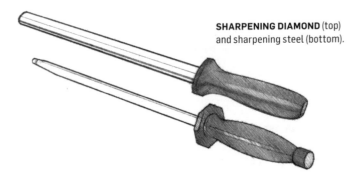

SHARPENING DIAMOND (top) and sharpening steel (bottom).

The sharpening diamond steel is also good for honing a sharp blade. It's similar to a sharpening steel, but has a diamond-crusted rough surface. Not only will it hone a blade, but it can also sharpen a somewhat dulled blade. Both of these tools are valuable to have.

How do you use these? Fortunately, the technique is the same for both tools. You can either stand the steel on its end, with its tip resting on a cutting board, or hold it by its handle, straight out in front of you. With the knife at a 22½-degree angle, slide the blade along the steel, from the handle end to the tip, at least five times for each side.

Start the blade at the handle end, at a 22½ degree angle.

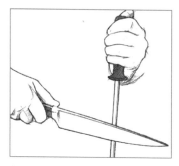

Slowly bring the knife down, while moving the blade until the tip is touching the steel.

Repeat the steps for the other side of the knife.

WHY CUTTING BOARDS MATTER

WHEN CHOOSING AMONG THE many types of available cutting boards, remember just one crucial thing: do not use a cutting board that has an extremely hard surface. This includes stone, glass, and boards made from manufactured countertop surfaces. Why manufactured countertop surfaces? This doesn't seem as obvious, but many people like to have cutting boards made from leftover scraps when they have new countertops installed in their kitchen. The problem with using these hard surfaces as cutting boards is that they'll quickly dull your knives' blades. You want a cutting board that has a little give to it.

The best materials for cutting boards are wood and polyethylene (usually called a poly board), which is a type of plastic. Both are solid, but not so hard that they'll dull your knives. They're porous, which also means they can be thoroughly cleaned. Although both types are very good, I prefer, and recommend, poly cutting boards over wooden ones because of how I like to clean them.

Cleaning

When you clean your cutting board, it's recommended that you wash it with dish soap and hot water. But it's also a good idea to run your boards through the dishwasher, or if you don't have a dishwasher, to soak your boards in the sink filled with water and a quarter of a cup of bleach. This will remove any stains and bacteria that might be lurking on your board. When you do this, make sure your kitchen is well ventilated.

Poly boards stand up to this kind of cleaning very well. Wooden boards, over time, will not hold up to soaking, bleaching, and visits to the dishwasher. Eventually, they'll crack and warp. However, wood does have natural bacteria-fighting properties, according to a 1993 study at the University of Wisconsin–Madison. Although these bacteria-fighting properties are not naturally found in polyethylene, bacteria can be destroyed through regular cleaning and bleaching. Also, wood cutting boards do need oiling on occasion, to keep them from becoming dry and brittle. Poly boards need no maintenance.

Slip Sliding Away

The most important thing I learned on my first day in cooking school was to put a damp cloth underneath my cutting board. This keeps your board from slipping and sliding on the counter. A damp piece of paper towel also works well. This is crucial because it's a safety issue: if your cutting board is moving, even a little bit, then your knife will move too. And if your knife, food, and cutting surface are all moving, then you've greatly increased your chance of cutting yourself. This little step will help.

Some boards have small suction cups or rubber feet on one side, which also help keep the board from sliding. I don't like these as much because this means that you can only use one side of the board. If you have a board that's smooth on both sides, then you have twice as much cutting board as the other ones. And if the board starts to warp, then you can turn it over to help it flatten out again.

How Many and What Size?

You don't want a board that's too small. It has to be big enough to hold whatever you're cutting, as well as your knife, plus a bit more space to give you some room to move things around as needed. It's also a good idea to have at least two or three boards. If you have only one board, a good size to have is 12 by 18 inches. This is big enough for small tasks, like cutting onions, or larger tasks, like carving a chicken.

If you have two boards, then it's also a good idea to keep one just for raw meats and seafood, and the other for vegetables and cooked foods. Another advantage of poly boards is that they come in all sizes and colors. The most popular ones are white. Some people like their boards to be in different colors to help keep them separate for raw meats and vegetables.

If you have three boards, then you'll always have one ready to use if the others are dirty in your sink or dishwasher.

CHAPTER FOUR

NONKNIFE, NONMOTORIZED SHARP KITCHEN TOOLS

Many kitchen tools aren't knives but are still very sharp. These can be just as valuable, but unlike knives, are often just task-specific. Over time, as you cook more, you'll buy these as you need them.

Vegetable Peeler

Vegetable peelers come in two different styles: the swivel style and the harp style (also called a Swiss or Y-style peeler). Like choosing a knife, it's a matter of what's comfortable in your hand. For that reason, my preference is the swivel-style peeler. But other people have told me they feel the same way about the harp style. If you're not sure, then you might want to buy both and see which you prefer. Different brands of each type of peeler range from $3 to $15. You can also spend almost $25 for a Swiss peeler that comes in right- and left-handed models. This, however, cuts down on the chances of having someone cook with you in your kitchen.

harp-style peeler

swivel-style peeler

The one thing to verify whenever you buy a peeler is that the blade is sharp. For some odd reason, some peelers are sharp, and stay that way for years, while others arrive dull, and are never very useful.

There is a rounded end on most swivel-style peelers to remove potato eyes and blemishes. It's easier and faster to use this rounded tip than to use a paring knife.

Scissors

Kitchen scissors are one of those tools that you don't realize you need until you need them. That sounds obvious, but they're more versatile and necessary than you might think. You need them for so many tasks such as cutting open food packaging, cutting the twine off raw and cooked meats, cutting through lobster and crab shells, and much more.

Cool Carrot Peeling Trick

In almost every class that I teach, I demonstrate a two-sided peeling technique, which works best with a swivel-style peeler. Carrots are perfectly shaped for this technique (parsnips too), but the surfaces of most other vegetables are too irregular.

Most people peel their carrots in single strokes, either drawing the peeler away from their body, or toward it. Since the peeler has a blade on both sides, the nifty trick is to hold the carrot at one end, and keep the peeler on the carrot. Peel back and forth, while rotating the carrot, without lifting the peeler. You can peel the carrot in half the time. This is especially helpful if you're a new line cook, as I was, and was instructed by the executive sous chef to peel a 25-pound bag of carrots. The task flew by with this cool technique.

If scissors are so important, why not go to the stationery store, buy a pair, and move on to the next thing? Because you need break apart (also called take-apart) scissors. What this means is that the two scissor halves come apart by opening them up all the way and separating them. This is crucial because it means that you can thoroughly clean and sharpen your scissors. This allows you to completely remove any raw or cooked food bits from the scissors' hinge. Without this, you'd be exposing yourself to harmful bacteria that will quickly build up in the scissors. Some scissors sold in the kitchenware section of stores and markets are not designed to be broken apart, so be sure to check before you buy.

Also, kitchen scissors must be used exclusively for food. Just as you don't want to use household scissors with food, you don't want to use your kitchen scissors for other household projects. In addition to being unsanitary, this can also dull the scissors.

Graters and Zesters

Until the mid-1990s, the main tool for grating and zesting was the box grater. This multipurpose monster could do everything: grate large and small shreds of carrots, cheese, or potatoes. Or create finer gratings of nutmeg, dry cheese, onions, or citrus zest. Box graters were typically made from metal, often aluminum, and usually grated two things: the food and your knuckles. The problem wasn't that the grater wasn't sharp. It was. The problem was that it wasn't sharp enough. When you'd grate food with it, you had to apply extra pressure on the food to allow it to grate. This usually led to a bit of slipping, and a grated knuckle.

Fast-forward to the mid-1990s, and the folks at Microplane accidentally revolutionized grating and zesting. They were making these tools for woodworkers and discovered the untapped market of shredded-knuckled cooks. With this discovery, Microplane became the standard for handheld zesters, graters, and even box graters. What they did was quite simple: they made these tools sharper and sturdier than before. This meant that cooks didn't have to apply extra pressure on the food to move along the sharp parts of the zester and grater.

This is particularly important when zesting citrus. Just below the outer skin of lemons, limes, oranges, and grapefruit lies the pith, the thin white layer that attaches to the fruit's flesh. The pith is bitter. With a Microplane zester, you could now remove the heavily scented and flavorful outer skin of the citrus without also accidentally removing the pith. While it's always been possible to remove zest with a traditional zester, that only did it in thin ribbons.

While Microplane isn't the only maker of zesters and graters, its products have become the standard that all others try to meet and exceed. There are other good brands available, including OXO, Zyliss, and KitchenAid.

In addition to zesting citrus, the smaller grater is good for finely grating Parmesan cheese, cinnamon sticks, nutmeg, fresh ginger, and more. A medium grater, which is shorter and wider, is good for grating ginger, carrots, chocolate, and whatever else

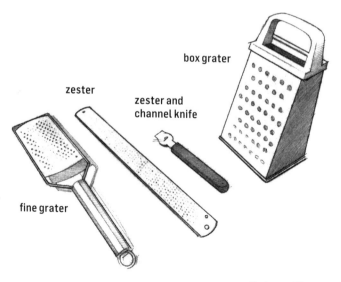

zester

box grater

zester and
channel knife

fine grater

you might want to grate. Oftentimes, if I'm making a dessert with freshly whipped cream, I'll grate dark chocolate over the whipped cream, the entire dessert, and the plate too. This always makes for a terrific, easy, and inexpensive dessert garnish.

I do still use a box grater for its largest grating function. It's perfect for carrots, cheese, and potatoes. Many of the zester and grater manufacturers make sharp, well-designed box graters for such tasks. But you still have to be very careful with your knuckles and pay close attention to what you're doing. The box graters are still like a magnet to your knuckles.

Mouli Grater

In the 1950s the French company Mouli came up with the coolest little gadget: a small handheld tool that had a crank, a hopper, and a shredding wheel. It became an instant hit with waiters and home cooks everywhere as a way to freshly grate cheese for hungry diners.

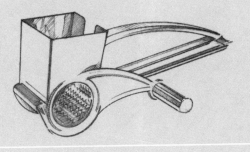

Mandoline

A mandoline is the most useful and dangerous nonknife tool you can have in your kitchen. Its sole purpose is to uniformly, without variation, cut vegetables. It's perfect if you want to create same-sized foods for uniform cooking, such as slicing potatoes to make French fries or potato chips. If all of the food is the same size, it will cook at the same rate. Or you may want the food to have a uniform look for display on a table or plate such as for a crudité, a cold vegetable and dip platter.

But a mandoline can be so dangerous that it's crucial to use it without any distractions or interruptions. Why is it more dangerous than a knife, or any other kitchen tool? First of all, the blade stays stationary and you move the food into it. This is similar to how we move food over the blades of zesters and graters, but the difference is that the blades on the mandoline are so large and sharp that you can easily do enough damage to yourself to require stitches, or worse. Although mandolines have hand guards in place, it is easy to slip and cut yourself on the blade.

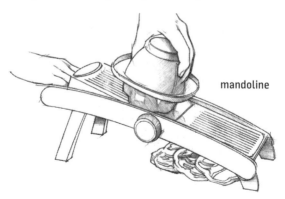

mandoline

The other reason a mandoline is so dangerous is because human nature and impatience often take over when using it. The hand guide that holds the food safely when you push it toward the blade is small and often awkward to use. And it can be difficult to clean. Human nature and impatience take over when cooks remove the guide and just use their hands to hold the food.

If you do feel compelled to remove the safety guide (this is dangerous and not recommended by anyone), use a cut-resistant glove on your guide hand. This will not guarantee that you won't cut yourself, but it will help if your hand grazes the blade. Different gloves are made from varying cut-resistant fibers, including Kevlar, which is used in bulletproof vests.

There are many brands and prices for mandolines, ranging from under $20 to over $200. I urge you not to buy a very cheap mandoline. With such sharp blades, you need to make sure the frame is solid and stable.

Mini Chopper

A mini chopper is a small version of a huge food processor, such as those made by Cuisinart, Robot Coupe, Viking, KitchenAid, and others. The vast majority of mini choppers are electric, just like their larger versions. Except the veggie chopper from Chef'n, which is not electric. This one has a pull string like a salad spinner, which spins the blades. It has a big ring at the top to pull the string, which is why some people call it the lawn mower chopper. It pulls just as though you were starting a lawn mower.

The mini chopper's advantage is its clever design. It has three very sharp blades. It's perfect for those tasks involving cutting smaller foods in larger quantities. It's great for chopping or mincing a bulb of garlic, an onion, or even chopping peanuts for your favorite pad Thai recipe.

Tomato Shark

Every now and then, a single-use tool comes along that makes itself invaluable. That's what the tomato shark did. But then I discovered that it has a second great use too. Its main purpose is to take the stem end out of a tomato. While a paring knife does this task well, it takes the knife a few movements and sometimes leaves an irregular and too-large hole in the top of your tomato. The shark will take the core out in one smooth motion, leaving a hole that's perfectly round and as shallow, or deep, as needed.

The shark's second function is that it's terrific at removing the tops from strawberries. It's better than a knife because it just takes off the green stem, and not too much of the edible berry.

But be careful. The tomato shark's teeth may be small, but it's still easy to snag your fingers on them. And we all know about shark bites.

tomato shark

Cheese Wire

This is one of the best inexpensive tools you can buy, and it is carried in many supermarkets. Most have a plastic roller just below the wire, which can be easily removed. This leaves you with a wire on a handle, ideal for slicing very soft cheeses, such as goat and blue. Both of these cheeses tend to break and crumble if you try to cut them with a knife.

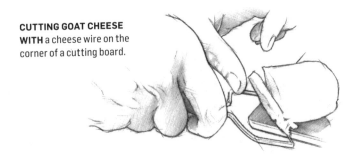

CUTTING GOAT CHEESE WITH a cheese wire on the corner of a cutting board.

When you use the cheese wire, place your cheese on the corner of the cutting board. This will allow the wire to come down onto the board and cut through the cheese completely. This is because the wire is just below the top of the handle, and it wouldn't otherwise cut entirely through the cheese.

Biscuit Cutter

Biscuit cutters come in two styles. The store-bought style often comes either in small boxes with multiple size cutters or as a single cutter. The other style is homemade and improvised, often the lid to a jar. An advantage of the purchased cutters is that they have a bit of a sharp edge. This means you'll be able to cut through not just dough, but fruit, vegetables, and sandwiches to create the special shapes that you want. They also come in round, fluted, and other shapes, whereas the lid from a jar is just round and only in a few sizes.

Pastry Wheel Cutters

These round bladed tools cut through thin dough, such as piecrusts, or simple dough, such as cheese straws. Pastry wheel cutters allow you to quickly and evenly cut your dough into pieces or strips. Yes, you can do the same thing with a paring knife by dragging it across the dough. But if you do that, you run the risk of cutting or scratching your countertop. Or worse, having uneven slicing. Plus, many pastry wheels have ridges, which give your dough a finished, fancier look. If you

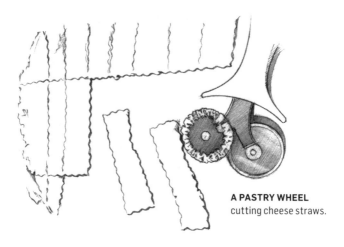

A PASTRY WHEEL
cutting cheese straws.

do this on your countertop, be aware that it may cause scratches. Consult your countertop manufacturer or owner's manual for their recommendations.

Pizza Cutter/Pizza Wheel

If you make your own pizza, this is a fun tool to have. Yes, it will make you feel like you're in a real pizza shop. But it's not a crucial tool to own. You can skip owning a pizza cutter and use your chef's knife instead to cut your pizza. Neither tool will improve, or detract from, the flavor of your homemade pizza masterpiece.

CHAPTER FIVE

RECIPES AND TECHNIQUES

From meat, poultry, and fish to vegetables, fruit, and even dessert, this section contains plenty of delicious ways to practice and improve your knife skills.

CARVING A TURKEY

I THINK THE BEST PLACE TO START is with the holiday that brings fear to so many people: Thanksgiving. This fear covers many aspects of the meal including preparing the menu, making the gravy, carving the turkey, and (sometimes) fending off relatives. But the main source of fear for many is carving the turkey. I can help you with this. But first, you'll need a few things to make sure your confidence level is high:

- A cutting board large enough to easily hold the turkey
- A 6-inch utility knife
- A damp paper towel or washcloth
- One large serving platter, or two smaller ones
- Extra paper towels
- A pair of metal tongs or carving fork
- Your kitchen counter

Do not carve the turkey at the table. Carve the turkey on a large cutting board (one that's at least 12 by 18 inches) on your kitchen counter. The countertop has a firm, stable surface, hopefully with some space available around it to hold your platter. A dining room table offers none of these. And in the dining room, everyone will be staring at you. And if it takes you more than 3 minutes to carve the turkey, and it will, the comments will be flying at you very quickly. If you drop any parts, or even the entire turkey, onto the table or the floor, then you and your descendants will be hearing about it until the end of time. That's why my Thanksgiving carving motto is "Bad things happen when there are witnesses. Always carve your turkey in the kitchen."

Set your cutting board on the counter with a damp paper towel placed underneath it. This will keep the board from slipping. Place a carving fork nearby to help you hold the turkey in place while you carve. A regular fork will also work, but not as easily. The 6-inch utility knife is the perfect size to work around the various parts of the bird. A chef's knife is too long for this task.

The next part is the actual carving, unless you have stuffing to remove. If so, do this first. Then you can start carving, keeping two things in mind: don't rush, and think of carving as being similar to taking apart a jigsaw puzzle. The parts that you're carving all fit together; with patience, the turkey will come apart easily.

You have eight things to carve: two legs (drumsticks), two wings, two thighs, and two breasts. Here's a logical order to follow:

First, the drumsticks. Gently cut around the base of the drumstick until you can see where the leg bone meets the thighbone. With the tip of your knife, you can easily cut away the connective tissue between the joints. You can see where the bones meet, and cut right there. The drumstick will come right off.

Removing the legs, wings, and thighs is very similar. For each of them, gently cut around the joint; that is, cut where the leg joins the thigh, where the wing joins the body, and where the thigh joins the body. As you cut around the joint, gently pull

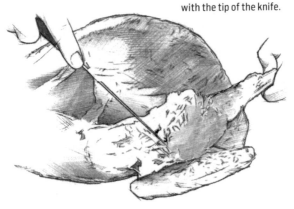

REMOVING THE DRUMSTICK
with the tip of the knife.

on the leg, wing, or thigh. The bone where the joints meet will show. Place the knife where they meet, and gently cut to separate them. Remove these bones before you remove the breast meat.

A variation of this step is to remove the thigh with the drumstick still attached. To do this, gently cut around the joint where the thigh attaches itself, just below the breast. The thigh will pull away, and you can easily see where the thighbone is connected. From here, you can detach the drumstick as described above. Do this with both drumsticks and thighs.

The next step is to remove the wings. To do this, flip the bird over. As with the drumsticks, gently cut the meat around where the wing is attached. It'll pull away, and you can easily cut the connective tissue where it attaches. The bone where the joints meet will show. Place the knife where they meet, and gently cut to separate them. Do this with both wings.

If you only removed the drumstick at this point, and not the thigh too, then you should now remove the thigh.

Now comes the removing and carving of the breast meat (the white meat). My preferred method is to remove the meat from the bone with a utility knife, in one large piece, and slice it into smaller pieces on your cutting board. To do this, hold the knife with the tip pointing down and look directly down at the turkey. At the top center, running the length of the turkey, is the breastbone that separates the two halves. Stick the knife into the meat, parallel to the breastbone, and as close to it as possible. Carefully cut the meat away from the bone, moving the knife all along the breast meat. Since you started in the center of the meat, cut the still-attached meat away, in the opposite direction you just cut. The meat will pull away from the bone, and you can cut whatever meat is still attached. The goal is

REMOVING THE WINGS
at the joint.

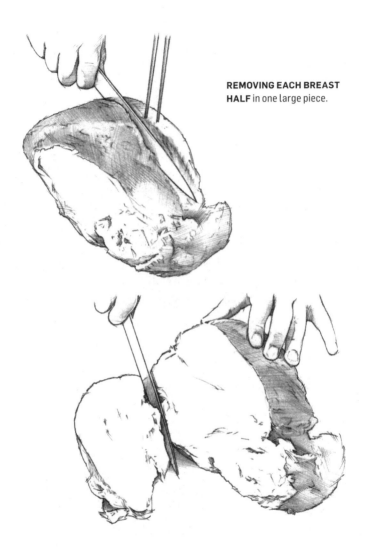

REMOVING EACH BREAST HALF in one large piece.

to remove each breast half in one piece. Cutting the length of breast meat, you can now cut slices in whatever thickness you'd like.

An alternate method is to leave the meat on the bone and carve long slices from it. For this method, you'll need a long slicing knife to make the slices as thin as you'd like. Using the utility knife will take quite a bit of effort to get the accuracy that you'll need. And a chef's knife may not give you the very thin slices that you might want.

I prefer the first method of removing all of the white meat in one piece. This is particularly true at Thanksgiving, as there's so much food on the table. To provide large slices almost always means people will not be able to eat all of the food on their plates. This leads to wasted food. With this method, you can easily and quickly carve slices that are the right size so your guests can take what they want, without wasting any food. This method also lets you carve the meat into more uniform slices, with the skin still attached. They can be as thick or thin as you'd like.

The remaining step is the easiest: place it all on the platter and serve!

Roast Turkey

For this recipe, you'll need a turkey roasting pan. If you don't have one and you use a disposable pan, make sure you place a sheet pan underneath it while roasting the turkey. This will help when you try to remove the turkey from the oven after it is cooked, as it might be unsteady.

 1 (18-pound) whole turkey
 8 cups (or more) stuffing
 ⅓ cup olive oil or softened unsalted butter
    salt and pepper
 2 cups turkey or chicken stock, or water

1. Remove the turkey from the fridge 1 hour before roasting to let it come to room temperature. Remove the neck and giblets, rinse the turkey, and pat dry with paper towels. Place the turkey, breast side up, on a rack in the roasting pan. If your roasting pan doesn't have a rack, you can place three to four whole carrots across the pan, and place the turkey on it. Or, you can roast the turkey directly in the pan, without carrots or a rack.

2. Preheat the oven to 325°F. Place the rack in the lowest position of the oven.

3. Just before roasting, loosely fill the body cavity with stuffing. Don't pack it in tightly as it may not cook all the way through. Brush the skin with the olive oil or melted butter, and generously season with salt and pepper.

4. Place the turkey in the oven, and pour 2 cups of stock into the bottom of the roasting pan. Baste every 30 minutes with the juices from the bottom of the pan. If the drippings evaporate, add more stock, 1 to 2 cups at a time.

5. Roast for 4 to 4 hours 30 minutes. If the skin is getting too browned before the turkey is done, place an aluminum foil tent, shiny side up, over the entire turkey. Roast until a meat thermometer inserted in the meaty part of the thigh reads 165°F.

6. Transfer the turkey to a large carving board and let it rest for 20 to 30 minutes before carving (see page 64).

Makes 9–12 servings

Tips for Turkey Success

- If your turkey comes with a plastic, pop-up thermometer already inserted in it, remove the thermometer and throw it away. The pop-up might not be 100 percent accurate. Instead, use an instant-read thermometer, inserted at the thigh, for an accurate temperature reading.

- Roasting time is approximately 15 minutes per pound for an unstuffed turkey and approximately 20 minutes per pound for a stuffed turkey. Previously frozen turkeys often take longer to roast than fresh ones. If you're roasting a turkey that had been frozen, make sure it's completely thawed before roasting.

- You don't have to tie up (truss) the legs for roasting. Trussing will not give you a moister turkey.

- You can make stock out of the giblets (neck, liver, heart, etc.), which are found either in the turkey's large cavity or in the smaller one at the opposite end of the large one, often under the skin. To make the stock, add 6 cups of water to the giblets, and add 1 onion, cut into quarters (you don't even have to peel the onion unless you want to), 2 carrots, cut into chunks (you don't have to peel the carrots, either), and 2 stalks of celery, including the leaves. Add 2 bay leaves (if you don't have these, it's okay to leave them out). Bring this to a boil, and gently simmer for 45 minutes. If the water level reduces by more than ⅓ cup, add more water. Strain, and you're ready to use the stock. You can make this up to 3 days ahead.

OTHER POULTRY, MEAT, AND FISH

UNLIKE A TURKEY, a roasted chicken is something that is fast to prepare throughout the year, and it can provide leftovers for days. It's also a great way to practice for your Thanksgiving turkey slicing since carving a chicken is almost the same as carving a turkey. In fact, most poultry are almost identical when it comes to carving. A duck has a slightly different skeletal structure, which slightly changes where some of the bones are attached. But the carving techniques remain the same.

Roast Chicken

This recipe is different than the others because the roasting pan is preheated. This gives the dark meat, on the bottom of the chicken, the opportunity to cook faster, and be fully cooked at the same time as the white meat.

> 1 (4–7 pound) whole chicken
> 1 onion, whole or cut in half
>   olive oil
>   salt, pepper, and paprika

1. Preheat the oven to 375°F.

2. Place a roasting pan or a cast-iron skillet, with nothing in it, in the preheated oven while you prepare the bird for cooking. Remove the giblets from the cavity of the bird. Put the onion in the cavity, and lightly oil the bird's skin. Sprinkle on salt, pepper, and paprika.

(continued on next page)

3. Carefully remove the heated pan or skillet from the oven, and place the bird in it.

4. Carefully put the chicken in the oven, and cook it for 15 to 20 minutes per pound, or until the bird is cooked through. The internal temperature of the chicken (check the temperature with an instant-read thermometer, at the thigh) should be 170°F.

5. When the chicken is cooked, remove it from the oven, and let it sit for 5 to 10 minutes, for the juices to settle.

Makes 6–8 servings

Curried Chicken

If you ask 20 cooks for a curried chicken recipe, you'll probably get 25 suggestions. It's so versatile and popular that you can add and subtract ingredients and still end up with a great dish.

2 tablespoons olive oil

2 onions, sliced

2–4 teaspoons curry powder

1½ pounds boneless, skinless chicken breast, cut into ½-inch slices or cubes, or 3 pounds boneless, skinless chicken thighs, cut into ½-inch slices or cubes

1 (14-ounce) can coconut milk (regular or light)

1 mango, peeled, pitted, and thinly sliced

¼ cup raisins

Tabasco (or other hot sauce) or red pepper flakes (optional)

salt and pepper

1. Heat a large skillet over medium-low heat. Add the oil and the onions and sauté for 15 to 30 minutes, or until the onions are browned and softened. The longer the onions cook, the softer and sweeter they'll be.

2. Add 2 teaspoons of the curry powder to the onions, turn the heat to medium-high, and stir for 30 seconds, or until they become fragrant. Add the chicken, and cook it until it's browned and partially cooked through, approximately 5 minutes.

3. Add the coconut milk to the chicken, and bring to a simmer. Add the mango and raisins, and simmer for 5 to 10 minutes, until it starts to thicken and the chicken is cooked through.

4. Taste the sauce and adjust the flavor as needed with curry powder, Tabasco, if using, salt, and pepper.

Makes 4 servings

Slicing Raw Boneless, Skinless Chicken Breast

To cube the chicken, cut the breast lengthwise into two or three strips, depending on the size that you want. Then cut the strips into cubes. This is great for stews and stir-fries.

The two cuts for the sliced and thinly sliced pieces are similar. To get these slices, cut the meat on the bias. In other words, slice diagonally across the meat rather than straight across. With any kind of food, including carrots and French bread, cutting on the bias will give you longer slices, which also give the food a nice visual appeal. To make these slices thinner for faster cooking such as stir-fry, slice the chicken breast in half and then cut your thin slices.

Cubed, sliced, and thinly sliced chicken.

Aunt Jean's Brisket

If you make this brisket a day in advance you can slice it when it's cold, which is easier, and skim any fat off the sauce. You can also freeze this after you cook it. Don't slice it before freezing, as this could make the meat a bit dry.

3–4	tablespoons canola or other vegetable oil (not olive oil)
3	large onions, sliced
2½-4-pounds	brisket, well trimmed of fat
	salt and pepper
1	cup ketchup
½	cup red wine
1	tablespoon steak sauce, such as A.1.
1	tablespoon soy sauce

1. Preheat the oven to 300°.

2. Add 2 tablespoons of the oil to a large ovenproof skillet (such as cast-iron), over medium heat, and sauté the onions until they are a golden color and cooked through. Try not to let them get too browned. A golden color is fine. This could take 20 or more minutes. Remove from the pan.

3. Turn the heat to high. Sprinkle the brisket with salt and pepper. Add the remaining oil to the pan. Brown the meat on all sides. This may splatter a bit, so be careful. Use a pair of tongs to hold the brisket up while you brown the narrow sides.

(continued on next page)

4. Combine the ketchup, red wine, steak sauce, and soy sauce. Pour the mixture over the browned brisket in the pan. The liquid should come approximately two-thirds of the way up the sides of the meat. If it appears a bit shallow, add more red wine.

5. Add the onions back into the pan and bring the liquid to a simmer.

6. Place the ovenproof skillet in the oven, and cook for 2 to 3 hours, or until the meat is very tender.

Makes 5–8 servings

Slicing Beef Brisket

The secret to a terrific beef brisket, other than the recipe, is slicing it against the grain. If you don't, then the meat can break into small pieces. This is because the meat is cooked for a long time, usually 2 to 3 hours, which causes the meat to be very tender and easily broken apart.

What does it mean to slice against the grain? As you look down onto the cooked meat, you can see the lines (this is the grain) and separations of the meat. They generally go in one direction. To make sure your knife is slicing in the right direction, hold your knife blade side down on the meat. The grain should be perpendicular to the knife. In other words, the grain should look as if it is heading into the side of the blade.

Haddock with Roasted Root Vegetables

This is a rustic, one-pan method to prepare fish and vegetables. The juices from the cooked fish give even more flavor to the classic roasted root vegetables. It's great in winter or on a rainy summer day.

- 4 red potatoes, cut into 2-inch pieces
- 2 carrots, peeled and sliced
- 2 onions, peeled and quartered
- 1 sweet potato or yam, peeled and cut into 2-inch pieces
- 1½ teaspoon salt
- ¾ teaspoon pepper
- ¼ cup plus 1 tablespoon olive oil
- 1½ pound haddock or cod, with the skin removed

1. Preheat the oven to 400°F.

2. Place the potatoes, carrots, onions, and sweet potato on a sheet pan, with 1 teaspoon of salt and ½ teaspoon black pepper. Toss with ¼ cup of the olive oil, and roast in the oven for 35 to 40 minutes, or until cooked through and browned. Turn the vegetables every 10 minutes to make sure they brown evenly. Remove from oven.

3. Increase the temperature to 425°F. Rub the fish with the remaining tablespoon of the olive oil, and season with the remaining ½ teaspoon salt and ¼ teaspoon black pepper. Place the fish on top of the vegetables and cook for 10 or so minutes, or until the fish is done to your liking.

Makes 4 servings

Removing the Skin from a Piece of Fish

The process of removing the skin from fish seems to go against common sense. That is, you'd think the skin would be on the top, and you'd slide a knife between the skin and the flesh. From experience, I can tell you that this almost never works. The actual process is the opposite. You need a cutting board, a knife that's at least a few inches longer than the width of the fish, and a piece of paper towel. This process applies to a single serving sized piece of fish, or a larger one, including a whole side of salmon.

With the fish placed skin side down, make a 1-inch slice between the skin and the flesh at either end of the piece of fish. With the paper towel in your guide hand, hold on to this flap of skin that you just created. That's where you'll insert the blade of your knife, not the tip. With your knife slightly angled so it's not parallel to the board, gently cut the skin from the flesh. With just a bit of practice, you'll find that this gets to be a simple step.

WITH THE FISH PLACED skin side down on the cutting board you can easily remove the skin.

Shrimp Pad Thai

For this recipe, the peanuts can be chopped as large or small as you'd like (using the mini chopper is faster than a chef's knife). If you are not going to be eating the pad Thai immediately, make extra sauce to ensure that if the noodles absorb all of the liquid, you'll have enough extra to keep them moist.

Fish sauce is available in the Asian section of most larger supermarkets. You can use honey or agave syrup in place of the sugar (if you use agave syrup, use 2 tablespoons instead of 3). You can also add tofu or chicken to the pad Thai.

- ½ pound pad Thai (rice) noodles
- ½ cup fish sauce
- ½ cup water
- 3 tablespoons sugar
- 1 lime, zest and juice
- 1 teaspoon paprika
- 6 dashes hot sauce
- 1–1½ tablespoons cooking oil
- 1 egg, beaten (optional)
- 1 pound shrimp, peeled and deveined
- ¼ cup peanuts, finely chopped
- 3 cloves garlic, minced
- 3 scallions, sliced
- ½ pound bean sprouts

1. Place the noodles in a large bowl, and cover with water for 30 to 45 minutes, or follow the package instructions. You

(continued on next page)

can even leave them for a few hours. They won't disintegrate. When the noodles are done soaking, drain and set aside.

2. Combine the fish sauce, water, sugar, lime zest and juice, paprika, and hot sauce in a bowl. Set aside.

3. If using the egg, add ½ tablespoon of the oil to a wok or large skillet, over medium heat, and cook the egg. Remove from the pan.

4. Increase the temperature to high. Add 1 tablespoon of the oil, and add the shrimp. Sauté the shrimp until it's cooked through, 2 to 3 minutes. Remove from the pan and set aside.

5. Turn the heat down to medium. Add 1 tablespoon of the peanuts and the garlic. Sauté for 10 to 20 seconds, or until the garlic becomes fragrant.

6. Add the noodles and the fish sauce mixture. Cover and cook for 2 to 3 minutes, or until the noodles are cooked to your liking. Check after 1 minute to make sure the noodles aren't sticking to the pan.

7. Add the egg and shrimp back into the pan to reheat.

8. Add the scallions and sprouts and combine. Remove from the pan, and place on a serving platter. Spread the remaining peanuts over the top, and serve.

Makes about 6 servings

Peeling Shrimp

Two methods for removing the shell and vein from shrimp involve a paring knife or a dull-edged shrimp deveiner tool.

If you're using a paring knife, pull off the shell with your fingers, and remove the vein by slicing down the back of the shrimp with the tip of the paring knife. This is often difficult, as the shell doesn't always come right off. It might come off in pieces, or not at all.

My preferred method is to use the dull-edged shrimp tool that does both tasks at once. Just push the tip between the shell and the flesh, and follow the contour of the shrimp. Occasionally, the vein along the back might not come out. If it doesn't, then use the tip of your paring knife to remove it.

FRUITS AND VEGETABLES

Tomato Salsa

Before chopping the cilantro, make sure all of the dirt is removed. To do this, soak it in a bowl of cold water. The dirt should come off and sink to the bottom of the bowl. At this point, taste the cilantro. If it's still gritty from dirt, soak it again, until it's grit-free. Dry the herbs in a towel, and chop them with your chef's knife using the method with your guide hand resting on top of the knife, near the end of the blade.

- 6–8 plum (or other) tomatoes
- ¼ cup fresh cilantro, minced
- ¼ medium red onion, finely chopped
- 3 scallions, chopped
- 2 tablespoons olive oil
- 2 tablespoons balsamic vinegar
- 1 tablespoon brown sugar
- 1 lime, zest only
-   salt and pepper
- 2 dashes hot sauce (optional)

1. Remove the green stem end of the tomatoes with a tomato shark or a paring knife. Chop the tomatoes into ½-inch pieces.

2. Combine the cilantro, onion, scallions, olive oil, vinegar, brown sugar, and lime zest with the tomatoes, and serve

chilled or at room temperature. *Note:* If you have approximately 30 minutes before you combine the salsa ingredients, place the chopped tomatoes into a strainer or colander, to drain off any excess liquid.

3. Before serving, adjust the flavor with salt, pepper, and hot sauce, if using. Serve with tortilla chips.

Makes about 1 quart

Preparing Garlic

Before slicing, chopping, or mincing garlic, follow two simple steps:

1. To remove the paperlike but very strong skin from the entire garlic bulb, rest it on its end, with the pointy part facing up. Place an open hand over the bulb, and place your other hand over that hand. Press down with all of your weight, or as much as you need, to break the outer skin of the bulb. The cloves will separate on your work surface.

2. To remove the outer skin from the individual garlic cloves, place a single clove under the flat part of your chef's knife blade. Press down on the blade with the palm of your hand until you hear the skin crack and give way. You can now remove the remaining skin with a paring knife and cut the garlic as needed.

Pesto

The fastest way to make pesto is in a food processor. If you don't have one, you can use a mini food chopper or a mortar and pestle, the original food processor. For additional flavor, add (any or all): sun-dried tomatoes, parsley, cilantro, anchovies (or anchovy paste), or roasted peppers.

- 2 cloves garlic
- 1 cup basil leaves, washed and dried
- ⅓ cup pine nuts (or other nuts)
- ¼ cup olive oil, plus extra as needed
- ¼ cup grated Parmesan cheese
- salt and pepper

1. Mince the garlic in a food processor.

2. Add the basil and pine nuts, and pulse until roughly chopped.

3. With the machine running, slowly add the ¼ cup olive oil until combined. If it's too dry, add more olive oil. It should be moist, but not swimming in oil.

4. Add the Parmesan and combine.

5. Season to taste with salt and pepper.

Makes ½ cup

Dorothy King's Coleslaw

To remove the core from a cabbage for coleslaw, cut the cabbage in quarters, down through the core. With a chef's knife or utility knife, cut out the exposed core. If you'd like, you can add a peeled, pitted, and thinly sliced mango to the coleslaw.

- 1 medium head green or red cabbage, shredded with a mandoline or finely chopped with a chef's knife
- 2–3 large carrots, peeled and grated
- 1 medium onion, grated finely
- ½ cup sugar
- ¼ cup distilled white or cider vinegar
- 1 teaspoon salt
- ½ teaspoon pepper

1. Combine the cabbage, carrots, and onion in a large bowl.

2. Whisk together the sugar and vinegar in a separate bowl until the sugar dissolves. Keep stirring. It's okay if the sugar doesn't dissolve completely. *Note:* If you want to dissolve the sugar, heat the vinegar and sugar mixture in a saucepan over medium heat until the sugar dissolves. Cool to room temperature before combining with the vegetables.

3. Pour the sugar mixture over the cabbage mixture. Season with salt and pepper. Chill for at least 30 minutes (or even better, overnight), and season to taste with salt and pepper.

Makes 10 servings

Everyday Fast Tomato Sauce

If you freshly grate Parmesan or Romano cheese, save the leftover rinds for when you make tomato sauce. Just add the rinds to the simmering sauce for extra flavor and remove what's left of them before you serve the sauce.

> 1 tablespoon olive oil
>
> 4 cloves garlic, minced
>
> 6–8 fresh tomatoes, peeled, seeded, and diced, or 1 (28-ounce) can diced tomatoes
>
> ¼ cup white wine
>
> 1 (6-ounce) can tomato paste (optional)
>
> 1 tablespoon dried basil or 2 tablespoons chiffonaded fresh basil
>
> salt and pepper

1. Add the olive oil to a saucepan over medium-high heat, and then add the garlic. Sauté for 20 seconds until it becomes fragrant. Add the tomatoes and wine and bring to a simmer. Add the tomato paste, if using, and simmer for 10 to 30 minutes, depending on how much time you have.

2. Add the basil, salt, and pepper and let simmer for another 5 minutes. Taste and adjust the salt and pepper as needed.

Makes approximately 1 pint

(3–4 servings)

The Chiffonade Cut

The chiffonade cut results in very thin, julienne-like strips and is used with large, leafy things such as sage, basil, and baby bok choy. To do this, take a few leaves (or as many as 10), and neatly stack them. Roll them up like a sleeping bag and then slice the roll, from one end to the other. This will look great in sauces and as a festive plate garnish.

A CHIFFONADE cut with basil.

Caesar Salad Dressing

This Caesar is unique because it does not have a raw egg yolk. Instead, the Parmesan, mustard, and anchovy paste help bind it together and give it the classic zesty flavor!

¼ cup vinegar (such as sherry, champagne, or cider)

4 anchovy fillets, rinsed and mashed, or 2 teaspoons anchovy paste

2 cloves garlic, minced

1 teaspoon mustard

2 tablespoons grated Parmesan cheese

2 dashes Worcestershire sauce

salt and pepper

½ cup olive oil

Cutting Lettuce for Caesar Salad

For romaine lettuce, make three cuts lengthwise in the lettuce, starting near the core. Rotate the lettuce one-third turn after each cut. Then cut the lettuce across those first cuts, almost all the way down to the core. It's best to wash and dry your lettuce after you've cut it. Drying is much easier when the lettuce leaves have been chopped, especially if you're using a salad spinner to thoroughly dry the lettuce.

Whisk together the vinegar, anchovy, garlic, mustard, Parmesan, Worcestershire, and salt and pepper. Slowly add the olive oil while whisking. Adjust the seasoning to suit your taste.

For a thicker dressing: Process the garlic in a blender. Add the vinegar, anchovy, mustard, Parmesan, Worcestershire, and salt and pepper. Slowly blend in the oil.

Makes approximately 1 cup

Potatoes au Gratin

Interpreted from a television chat between Jacques Pépin and Julia Child, this is a rustic version of a gratin. It doesn't have cheese, cream, or bread crumbs. It gets its browned crust just from baking in the oven.

2	tablespoons olive oil
2	onions, sliced
4 or 5	Yukon gold or red bliss potatoes, cut into ¼-inch slices with a mandoline or chef's knife (peeling is optional)
1	teaspoon salt
½	teaspoon black pepper
2	cups (approximately) chicken stock

1. Preheat the oven to 375°F.

2. Heat a large cast-iron skillet over medium/medium-low heat. Add the olive oil and then the onions. Sauté for 15 to 20 minutes, or until they start to brown and soften. You can sauté the onions for longer, even caramelizing them for more

(continued on next page)

flavor. *Note:* If you don't have a cast-iron skillet, or an oven-proof skillet, heat the potatoes on the stove top in a skillet. Then, carefully transfer the hot mixture to an ovenproof dish, such as a pie plate, to bake in the oven.

3. Add the potatoes, salt, and pepper. Add enough stock to barely cover the potatoes and bring to a simmer. When the mixture has reached a simmer, remove the skillet from the stove top, and place in the oven, uncovered.

4. Bake for 35 to 45 minutes, or until the stock is absorbed and a crust begins to form on the potatoes. If some stock remains in the pan, that's okay. Either remove it before serving, or serve it with the liquid. Both work well.

Makes 4–6 servings as a side dish

Guacamole

Making guacamole allows plenty of room for experimentation. Although plum tomatoes are preferred because they're firmer and less juicy than most other tomatoes, any fresh tomatoes will work well. Feel free to use more or fewer tomatoes than the recipe specifies. If you use more tomatoes, then you'll have a higher yield of guacamole, which will be helpful if unexpected guests arrive. You can also add sour cream to make the guacamole a bit richer and more flavorful. It's smart to taste the guacamole after you've put in one dash of the hot sauce. While this isn't a superspicy recipe, this might be enough for you.

A ripe avocado should be barely soft to the touch. The outer color may vary, some being black or brown, and others a dark green. The most popular type is the Hass avocado, which has an almost black skin when ripe. An avocado that's not yet ripe will be quite hard and mostly green. It could take 3 to 5 days to ripen. To help speed up the ripening, place the avocados in a brown paper bag on your counter, and check them each day for ripeness. If they get ripe before you want to use them, put them in the refrigerator for 1 or 2 days.

- 2 ripe avocados, peeled, with pits removed
- 4 plum tomatoes, chopped, with stem ends removed
- 1 lime, zest only
- 2 cloves garlic, minced, or ¼ teaspoon garlic powder
  salt
- 1–2 dashes hot sauce

1. Place the avocados in a large bowl, and mash with a fork or a potato masher, until the lumps are gone.

2. Mash in the tomatoes, lime zest, garlic, salt, and hot sauce, and serve immediately with tortilla chips or other chip or cracker. If you make the guacamole up to an hour ahead, store it in the refrigerator covered with plastic wrap. Make sure the plastic wrap is resting right on the surface of the guacamole, and not above it. This will help keep the guacamole from turning brown. If it does start to turn brown, just skim off the brown top before serving.

Makes about 1 quart

Pitting an Avocado

To pit an avocado, follow these simple steps:

1. Remove the tiny stem end on the small tip of the avocado with your fingers. It'll pull right off. With the avocado resting on its side, place your hand, palm down, on top of the avocado to keep it from rolling around.

2. With a chef's knife, gently slice lengthwise through the skin (the avocado's, not yours) to the large, round pit, and rotate the avocado until it's sliced all the way around.

3. Separate the two halves. Place the half, pit side up, in the palm of your hand, with your hand wide open. Don't wrap your fingers around the avocado half.

4. Gently, let the knife blade, at the middle, drop onto the pit. You don't have to give it any extra momentum. When it sticks a bit into the pit, give the knife a slight turn, and the pit will pop out. If the avocado is slightly underripe, it might take two tries to remove the pit, which might stick a bit to the fleshy green part.

THE CORRECT WAY to hold an avocado for slicing and removing the pit.

BAKED GOODS

Baby Brownies from the
New Basics Cookbook
by Julee Rosso and Sheila Lukins

The best knife to cut into brownies is a plastic, disposable knife. The serrated teeth are small enough to cut the brownie crust without shattering it, as most other knives will do. It's best to do this while the brownies are still warm.

- 6 ounces semisweet chocolate
- ¼ cup chocolate syrup
- 8 tablespoons (1 stick) unsalted butter, at room temperature
- 1 teaspoon vanilla extract
- 2 eggs, lightly beaten
- ¾ cup sugar
- ⅛ teaspoon salt
- ½ cup all-purpose flour

1. Preheat the oven to 350°F. Grease (butter or spray) and flour an 8-inch square baking pan. Set it aside.

2. Melt the chocolate using a double boiler or microwave. Add the syrup after the chocolate is melted. Stir well. Remove the pan from the heat, and add the butter. Beat until the mixture is smooth. Stir in the vanilla and eggs. Mix thoroughly.

(continued on next page)

3. In a mixing bowl, sift or whisk together the sugar, salt, and flour. Add this to the chocolate mixture and blend thoroughly.

4. Pour the batter into the pan, and bake until just cooked, approximately 30 minutes.

5. After the brownies have cooled for 5 minutes, cut them to the desired size. You can wait until they're cool, but the top will get crusty and they won't cut evenly.

Makes 1–20 servings

(depending on your appetite)

Preparing Fruit

To remove the rind (also called the skin or peel) from a pineapple, melon, cantaloupe, or other similar fruit, cut the ends off the fruit, and stand it on one of the now-flat ends. With an offset handle serrated knife, carefully cut from top to bottom to remove the rind. You can now cut the fruit in any way that you'd like.

The supreme cut for citrus is done to remove the individual segments without including the chewy membrane that's between each segment. This cut is used for salads, desserts, and anytime you want to give a finished look and a better mouthfeel to the food.

To do a supreme cut, cut the top and bottom skin off the citrus with a utility, paring, or offset handle serrated deli knife. Then, with the citrus resting on one of its now-flat sides, cut off the skin, as well as the inner white layer (the pith). Hold the citrus so you can see the wedges and the membranes surrounding them. Cut between each membrane with a paring knife to remove each wedge.

THE STEPS TO a supreme citrus cut.

Ernest Dzendolet's Lithuanian Lightning Cake

This simple cake is also an easy and tasty way to practice cutting something round. Try frosting the cake with your favorite chocolate icing or sprinkle confectioners' sugar over the top. You can also serve it with a sauce (such as peach, raspberry, or lemon curd) or with freshly whipped cream.

    1 cup all-purpose flour
    1 cup sugar
    1 teaspoon baking powder
    ¼ teaspoon salt
    4 tablespoons (½ stick) butter
    2 large eggs
      milk
    1 teaspoon vanilla

1. Preheat the oven to 400°F. Grease (butter or spray) and flour an 8-inch or 9-inch round cake pan.

2. Whisk together the flour, sugar, baking powder, and salt.

3. Melt the butter in a glass liquid measuring cup. Lightly beat the eggs, and add them to the butter. Add enough milk to this mixture so it totals 1 cup in volume.

4. Add the butter mixture to the dry ingredients, and combine until well mixed. Mix in the vanilla.

5. Bake for 30 minutes, or until a cake tester or toothpick comes out dry from the center of the cake.

6. Cool for five minutes before removing from the pan.

Makes 1 single-layer cake

Cutting Pies or Cakes

Knowing how to cut a pie or cake (or any round food, such as pizza or cheese) into even pieces is important for two reasons. One is that you'll know exactly what your yield will be. Do you want to be the one to tell the 12th guest that there are only 11 slices of cake? The other reason is appearance. If you just start cutting wedges, the first two will look terrific. After that, they'll all look lopsided. It's almost impossible to get uniform, attractive pieces from random cutting. Your guests will thank you for your nice-looking, perfectly cut, equally sized wedges.

The first step is to cut the circle in half. Then cut each half in half. You now have four quarters. From the pointy end of each quarter, rest your knife to cut as many pieces as you need. For instance, three pieces per quarter will give you a total of 12 pieces.

HOW TO CUT ROUND FOOD

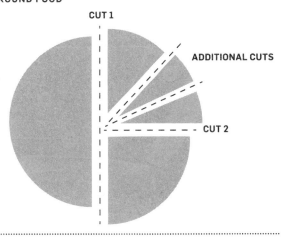

Cheese Straws

Use a fluted pastry wheel to get a finished look with the cheese straws.

¼ pound (about 1½ cups) coarsely grated extra-sharp cheddar cheese

1 cup all-purpose flour

¾ stick (6 tablespoons) cold unsalted butter, cut into small pieces

½ teaspoon salt

⅛ teaspoon cayenne pepper

½ tablespoon milk

1. Preheat the oven to 350°F.

2. In a food processor, pulse the cheese, flour, butter, salt, and cayenne until the mixture resembles coarse meal. Add the milk and pulse until the dough forms a ball. You can also combine all of the ingredients with your hands.

3. Roll out the dough on a lightly floured surface with a lightly floured rolling pin into a 12- by 10-inch rectangle (⅛ inch thick). Cut the dough with a pastry wheel into ½- by 2-inch strips, or any shapes that you like.

4. Carefully transfer to an ungreased baking sheet, arranging the strips ¼ inch apart. (If any strips tear, pinch them back together.)

5. Bake until pale golden, 15 to 18 minutes.

6. Cool completely on the baking sheet on a rack, about 10 to 15 minutes. These will keep for 3 days in an airtight container.

Makes about 3 dozen cheese straws

Metric Conversion Chart

Unless you have finely calibrated measuring equipment, conversions between U.S. and metric measurements will be somewhat inexact. It's important to convert the measurements for all of the ingredients in a recipe to maintain the same proportions as the original.

General Formula for Metric Conversion

Ounces to grams	multiply ounces by 28.35
Grams to ounces	multiply grams by 0.035
Pounds to grams	multiply pounds by 453.5
Pounds to kilograms	multiply pounds by 0.45
Cups to liters	multiply cups by 0.24
Fahrenheit to Celsius	subtract 32 from Fahrenheit temperature, multiply by 5, then divide by 9
Celsius to Fahrenheit	multiply Celsius temperature by 9, divide by 5, then add 32

Approximate Equivalent by Volume

U.S.	METRIC	U.S.	METRIC
1 teaspoon	5 milliliters	2 cups	460 milliliters
1 tablespoon	15 milliliters	4 cups (1 quart)	0.95 liter
½ cup	120 milliliters	1.06 quarts	1 liter
1 cup	230 milliliters		

Approximate Equivalent by Weight

U.S.	METRIC	METRIC	U.S.
½ ounce	14 grams	1 gram	0.035 ounce
1 ounce	28 grams	50 grams	1.75 ounces
1½ ounces	40 grams	100 grams	3.5 ounces
2½ ounces	70 grams	250 grams	8.75 ounces
4 ounces	112 grams	500 grams	1.1 pounds
8 ounces	228 grams	1 kilogram	2.2 pounds
16 ounces (1 pound)	454 grams		

RESOURCES

Cliver, Dean O., and Nese O. Ak.
"Study: Wood Cutting Boards, Not Plastic, Are Safer for Food Prep," University of Wisconsin, January 1993.

Elliot, Jeffrey, and James P. DeWan.
The Zwilling J. A. Henckels Complete Book of Knife Skills: The Essential Guide to Use, Techniques & Care. Robert Rose, 2010.

Rosso, Julee, and Sheila Lukins.
The New Classics Cookbook. Workman, 1989.

Casco Bay Cutlery & Kitchenware
800-646-8430
http://freeportknife.com

Chef'n
206-448-1210
www.chefn.com

Different Drummer's Kitchen
413-586-7978
www.differentdrummerskitchen.com

Microplane
800-555-2767
www.microplane.com

Stonewall Kitchen
800-826-1752
www.stonewallkitchen.com

Williams-Sonoma, Inc.
877-812-6235
www.williams-sonoma.com

ACKNOWLEDGMENTS

My mom, Carol, who will (and does!) tell everyone that she was my first cooking teacher. And my late dad, David, who loved to cook the foods of his native England, and taught me to love Marmite, kippers, and chopped herring.

My sister Bea. Every conversation with her, on the phone or in person, ends up being about food. And my sister Scott, who's been creating vegetarian cuisine forever.

Michael Palmer, the awesome *New York Times* best-selling thriller writer. He quickly morphed from being a client to a friend to family. And Robin Broady, who loves my food with Michael.

Ernest Dzendolet, my late father-in-law. He was a self-taught cook, who loved to talk to me about food, knives, gadgets, and all things culinary. He called me his personal chef before I ever became one.

And my friends who are family: Mollye Wolahan and Todd Lockwood, and their love and appreciation of my food; Thomas Cowern and Larry Layton, who inspired me to go to cooking school; Henry Kanter, who will gratefully eat anything, even the food I cooked in college.

Joan Parker, the awesome literary agent who understands me better than I do.

Doug and Rhoda Dillman, from Casco Bay Cutlery and Kitchenware in Freeport, Maine. Their help and huge knowledge of knives have been so important not just in writing this book, but for so much help and information for many years.

Dennis Greco, from Different Drummer's Kitchen and Cook's Resource in Northampton, Massachusetts. His generosity of time and knife skills were terrific.

The truly gracious and easy-to-work-with people at Storey Publishing, especially Margaret Sutherland, Matt LaBombard, and Mollie Firestone.

Jim and Jonathan, and all of the cooking school folks at Stonewall Kitchen in York, Maine. Their help and easy style make their cooking school the best around.

Atkins Farms Market, in Amherst, Massachusetts, whose dedication to food and teaching have made them a regional destination for decades, and a great place for my cooking lessons.

INDEX

Page numbers in *italic* indicate illustrations; numbers in **bold** indicate charts.

oyster knife, 26–27, *27*

P

Pad Thai, Shrimp, 81–82
paring knife, 14–15
   as essential, 3, 4, *4*
   holding, 15, *15*
   for peeling shrimp, 83
pastry wheel cutters, 61–62, *61*
Pesto, 86
pies, cutting, 99, *99*
pith, 55, 97
pizza cutter/pizza wheel, 62, *62*
poly cutting boards, 48, 49, 50
potatoes
   grating, 54, 56
   Potatoes au Gratin, 91–92
   removing eyes from, 52
   slicing, 57
poultry. *See also* chicken; duck;
      turkey
   boning, 21
   carving, 17
pull-through sharpeners, 43, *43*
purchasing knives. *See* buying
      a knife

R

Roast Chicken, 73–74
Roasted Root Vegetables,
      Haddock with, 79
Roast Turkey, 70–71
round food, how to cut, 99, *99*

S

salami, 14
salmon, slicing, 24
Salsa, Tomato, 84–85
sandwiches, cutting, 17
Santoku knife. *See* Japanese
      Santoku knife
scallop knife, 26–27
scissors, 52–54
sharpening knives, 42–47
   pull-through sharpeners,
      43, *43*

sharpening services, 33
sharpening steel/sharpening
      diamond steel, 46–47,
      46, 47
   whetstone and, 44–45, *45*
shellfish, knives for, 26–27, *27*
shopping online, 34–35
shrimp
   peeling, 83
   Shrimp Pad Thai, 81–82
slicer, 23–24
sliding technique, chef's knife
      and, 10, 12, *12*
specialty knife stores, 33
spices, grating, 54, 55
spoon, 27–28
stamped knives, 36
steak knives, 23
steel
   high carbon stainless, 36
   Japanese and German, 37
strawberries
   hulling, 14
   removing tops from, 59
supreme cut, 14, 97, *97*
Swiss peeler, 51–52
swivel-style peeler, 51, *52*

T

tang, *5*, 39
   handle and, 39, 40
tip of knife, *5*
tomatoes
   coring, 14
   Everyday Fast Tomato
      Sauce, 88
   peeling, *15*
   slicing, 17, *18*
   Tomato Salsa, 84–85
tomato shark, 59–60, *59*
transferring chopped foods, 19, *19*
turkey. *See also* carving a turkey
   Roast Turkey, 70–71
   slicer for, 23
   tips for success, 72

U

utility knife, 16–17, *16*

V

vegetable peeler, 51–52
vegetables. *See also* specific
      vegetable
   cutting board for, 50
   Haddock with Roasted Root
      Vegetables, 79
   slicing, 4

W

washing knives, 39–40
"whet," term, 44
whetstone, 44–45, *45*

Y

Y-style peeler, 51–52

Z

zesters, 54–56, *55*